"In his usual eminently readable style, Thomas O'Loughlin presents forceful arguments on why Christians from different churches should share in communion with one another as they journey [illegible] serious reflection."

—Paul F. Bradshaw
University of Notre Dame

"In this engagingly written book, Thomas O'Loughlin conducts a compelling theological exploration of a persistent and unresolved question in pastoral life. A series of reflections on what it means for Christians to 'eat together' at the eucharist draw with equal poise on canon law, profound readings of scripture, and the experience of parish life. Both systematic teaching and challenge, they lead readers of all churches to reimagine local reality, and live it differently, in the light of the imperatives of the kingdom."

—Bridget Nichols
Lecturer in Anglicanism & Liturgy, Church of Ireland Theological Institute, Dublin

"Development in doctrine or ecclesial practice is a fact throughout the history of the Catholic Church. Often such changes have come about through taking a fresh perspective on a particular issue. In this carefully argued book, Thomas O'Loughlin presents a compelling case for change in Catholic practice regarding eucharistic hospitality. O'Loughlin writes as a historian, theologian, liturgist, and pastor; but it is above all his pastoral perspective that gives his call for change such cogency and urgency."

—Ormond Rush, author of *The Vision of Vatican II: Its Fundamental Principles*

"Do not be deceived. This book is about a lot more than eucharistic sharing among Christians. It is indeed about sharing communion, but O'Loughlin also provides excellent ecumenical and eucharistic theology to back up his bold proposals for Catholic eucharistic hospitality. We desperately need this kind of forward-looking thinking today. I recommend it highly to pastoral ministers, theologians, and ministerial students—in fact to anyone concerned with the issue of eucharistic sharing."

—John F. Baldovin, SJ
Boston College School of Theology and Ministry

Discard

APR 24 '24

Eating Together, Becoming One

Taking Up Pope Francis's Call to Theologians

Thomas O'Loughlin

Library St. Vincent de Pau
10701 S. Military Trail
Boynton Beach, Fl 33436

LITURGICAL PRESS
ACADEMIC

Collegeville, Minnesota
www.litpress.org

Cover design by Monica Bokinskie.

Cover image: This painting entitled *Das Abendmahl unter Tage* [The Eucharist Underground] is a piece of public art on an underpass in the town of Westerholt in North Rhein-Westphalia, Germany. It was painted in 2011 by Helmut Dellmann, who died April 18, 2013, and who was a founding member of the local miners' old-comrades' association that now cares for the painting. It presents the eucharist not only as an activity of the people of God in union with Jesus but as an incarnational event. Rather than occurring in a sacred space apart from the world, it enters into the workspace and transforms that location into a place of divine encounter and an experience of community rejoicing.

Scripture quotations are from *New Revised Standard Version Bible* © 1989 National Council of the Churches of Christ in the United States of America. Used by permission. All rights reserved worldwide.

Excerpts from the English translation of *The Roman Missal* © 2010, International Commission on English in the Liturgy Corporation. All rights reserved.

© 2019 by Order of Saint Benedict, Collegeville, Minnesota. All rights reserved. No part of this book may be used or reproduced in any manner whatsoever, except brief quotations in reviews, without written permission of Liturgical Press, Saint John's Abbey, PO Box 7500, Collegeville, MN 56321-7500. Printed in the United States of America.

1 2 3 4 5 6 7 8 9

Library of Congress Cataloging-in-Publication Data

Names: O'Loughlin, Thomas, author. | Francis, Pope, 1936–
Title: Eating together, becoming one : taking up Pope Francis's call to theologians / Thomas O'Loughlin.
Description: Collegeville : Liturgical Press, 2019. | Includes bibliographical references and index. | Summary: "Explores various ways of thinking about what Catholics do in the liturgy that should lead us to see intercommunion between Christian denominations as enhancing our participation in the mystery of the Church and the mystery we celebrate"—Provided by publisher.
Identifiers: LCCN 2019013420 (print) | LCCN 2019980258 (ebook) | ISBN 9780814684580 (pbk.) | ISBN 9780814684832 (ebook)
Subjects: LCSH: Lord's Supper—Catholic Church. | Lord's Supper.
Classification: LCC BX2215.3 .O46 2019 (print) | LCC BX2215.3 (ebook) | DDC 264/.02036—dc23
LC record available at https://lccn.loc.gov/2019013420
LC ebook record available at https://lccn.loc.gov/2019980258

For Daniel Rossa
—a token of gratitude

"But be doers of the word, and not merely hearers"
—James 1:22

Contents

Preface

The idea of this book can be traced to a few off-the-cuff remarks that were made in a Lutheran church in Rome in November 2015, when Pope Francis replied to a question about intercommunion and suggested that theologians should address the question! I had by then lost count of how many times I had been asked a version of that question in churches, in class, in meetings with clergy, and even once while waiting for a plane in India: Why will the Catholic Church not allow other Christians, whom they acknowledge as Christian, to share their table? I then recalled that I could not think of a single book that presented the arguments in favor of a change in Catholic practice—the very sort of examination Pope Francis was calling for. So the idea took root, and I desired a small book that would address the several dimensions of the question (theological, liturgical, and pastoral) in a unified way. This, what you hold in your hand, is the result.

But even a small book runs up a large list of debts of gratitude. First and foremost, I am grateful for the questions and stimulating seminars that have taken place with those undergraduates in the University of Nottingham who over the last decade have taken my "History of the Eucharist" module. Coming from every denomination, several faiths, and sometimes no faith background but an interest in the human phenomenon of religion, they have asked me a range of questions to which few theologians who write on worship are exposed. I am in their debt more than they realize. While speaking of Nottingham I am also in the debt of my colleagues—it is a department of friends—who patiently have helped me clarify my thoughts on many matters.

Second, I need to thank all those communities of Christians who have asked me to speak to them about the eucharist. While it would be expected that I would be invited to speak to Catholic dioceses and groups, I have also learned so much from being asked to address what it is we are doing when we are eucharistic with many other churches. I must single out for mention just a couple of them because their welcome has left such a memory with me: the Episcopal seminary of Nashotah House in Wisconsin, the Countess of Huntington Connection Chapel in Mortimer, West End, in Berkshire, and a United Church of Canada in Victoria on Vancouver Island. The eucharist does really unite us because we recognize our need to be thankful to the Father, and we know that sharing food binds us as human beings.

Immediately following the pope's statement, the Franciscan Sisters in Arkley (to the north of London) organized a special one-day conference on the topic drawing together Anglican and Catholic scholars in February 2016—they moved fast—and conversations at the seminar with Bridget Nichols, now president of the Societas Liturgica, James Cassidy, and Patricia Rumsey (abbess of Arkley and the moving spirit behind that seminar) convinced me that a book was needed. For all the work involved in organizing that fruitful seminar, we are all indebted to that community. But it was not until I was speaking with an even wider range of scholars at the 2017 Leuven meeting of Societas Liturgica that I became fully convinced that this was a worthwhile project. For all their inspiration and encouragement I am in their debt. In the aftermath of that conference I approached Liturgical Press and am now also indebted to Hans Christoffersen—who has taken the lead on the project—and all the staff there.

I would like to thank Daniel Rossa, once my Erasmus student in Nottingham, for drawing my attention some years ago to the stunning painting by Helmut Dellmann's *Das Abendmahl unter Tage* on the cover and for taking the photograph of that painting. I am grateful to Kunibert Kiehne of the Knappenvereins "St. Barbara" Bergmannsglück in Westerholt for permission to reproduce the image—and, once again, to Daniel for obtaining this permission for me.

I would also like to thank John Bolger, then editor of *One in Christ* for pushing forward the publication of the 2016 seminar; to Brendan Walsh, editor of *The Tablet*, for encouraging the project as an urgent one; and, yet again, to Patricia Rumsey for agreeing to read the typescript and save me from split infinitives. What is written here takes a very definite line within the broad tradition of Catholic theology, and so for the opinions found here—and for the blunders that remain—I alone am responsible.

Introduction

A Problem for Pastors and Theologians

One of the great signs of hope in the Christian world over the past century has been the growth of the ecumenical movements as churches saw discourse rather than discord as the more appropriate tone for their mutual relationships. Then in the 1960s, part of the overall renewal of the Second Vatican Council, the Roman Catholic Church entered these dialogues, and old enmities were set aside and new relationships established. The joy of seeing Patriarch Athenagoras I and Pope Paul VI embracing on the Mount of Olives in January 1964 was often matched at local level by the first time a group of Catholics, ever so tentatively, went inside a local Protestant church for an ecumenical service. Learning to be with one another and learning to pray together was a slow and often tense business; and the idea of learning *from* one another was not even considered. In many places sectarianism was still just beneath the surface—and it has still not disappeared—but slowly we Christians are discovering one another not as strangers but fellow pilgrims.

As we progressed we also discovered that, if we are serious about ecumenism, it is more demanding of change within ourselves than an annual special occasion during Church Unity Week or admiring some carefully nuanced joint statement relating to historic divisions. If we were serious, then being pilgrims together meant that we had to share those things that are supposed to be precious among Christians, and here we ran into trouble immediately over that very reality that is supposed to bind us together: the eucharist. The sacrament of unity was actually the lightening rod of division! This separated the Western churches, Protestants and

Catholics, from one another, and separated the Catholics and the Orthodox from one another. There have been documents on this from the churches aplenty, no end to special workarounds, but eucharistic intercommunion is more than a mere roadblock. Knowing it is such a barrier to full communion often "takes the wind out of the sails" of those who work for the unity for which Jesus prayed (John 17:11). Often faced with this conundrum, church leaders and theologians adopt the line of "do what you can," knowing that there is a pre-set limit to growth (unless one church simply converts to the other) saps energy. We look back on the photographs of the various embraces of church leaders and place them alongside other handshake images—such as that of Yasser Arafat and Yitzhak Rabin on the White House lawn in September 1993—that were full of promise and good intention but led nowhere.

But sharing at the eucharist is not simply a matter for theologians or leaders; it will cause pain and division next Sunday in a church somewhere near you. It will be the pain of a family arguing about being together at what many churches would describe as the center and summit of the Christian life. It will cause hurt and new dissention when a pastor prevents or reproves a fellow Christian from sharing at the Lord's gracious banquet. And, sadly, for many Catholics it is seen as a closed issue—or one that is so fraught with difficulties that it is best ignored. This book argues that it is an issue we Catholics need to confront openly not just in reflection but, as befits anything concerning the eucharist as a form of Christian activity, in what we do.

What follows is not a single supposedly "knockdown argument" in favor of a change in Catholic practice but a series of theological reflections: each a glimpse strung together as a chain. In all such matters of practical theology, the evidence from all our sources of theology scripture, doctrine, law, practice, ritual, art, history, and so on is hardly ever so clear and one-sided that it can clear opposition from the field. Rather, it is a case that the wider sweep of theological sense, the *sensus ecclesiae*, suggests that we have reached a tipping point and that we need to alter our practice. Then, sensing that this is the correct way forward, we need to see how this can be seen to be in accord with our tradition. The chapters that follow each approach the issue from a different angle, but when taken together they provide, I hope, a cumulative case for a change in practice.

When I am in the process of writing a book, one question is always unwelcome: What are you working on now? I may have only just begun and wonder if I am really engaging, or I could be close to the end and wonder if I will have the energy to bring it to a conclusion. And there is always the doubt as to whether one has adequately addressed the relevant questions. So when such a question is asked, I usually fudge. Within days of completing this manuscript, I was again asked this question around a table that included several Catholic clergy, so I felt confident to give a rather definite answer: a book taking up the question of Pope Francis to theologians on intercommunion. To my shock and sadness one of the presbyters quipped: "I don't know why we should bend over to them until they give us something!" I had, perhaps naively, imagined that we had moved beyond the tit-for-tat view of relations between churches as a kind of political game. Thinking about it, I realized that the importance of intercommunion is not that it might be an action that might promote good ecumenical relations (which it would) or even that it would bring solace to painful pastoral situations (which it will) but because it is the right thing to do. I hope that I have shown that it is out of the inherent nature of our liturgy that intercommunion is a good to be pursued. It is certainly my own conviction that intercommunion is not a matter of church relations but a witness to the nature of the new covenant that has been established with us in the Christ. We share because he has already made us one in him in our baptism.

I have been concerned with this issue of sharing at the eucharistic table since I first met it as a real pastoral issue in the early 1980s, and over the years I have tried to tease out in academic papers some of its dimensions.[1] Then came the call from Pope Francis in late 2015 for theologians to review the issue afresh and some very insightful off-the-cuff notes on how such a review might take place.[2] Reading the pope's statement I at once tried to reshape some work I had recently published on the topic,[3] and then asked a small group of theologians to look at it and the results were published in a special issue of *One in Christ*.[4] Then at a meeting of

1. For instance, O'Loughlin 2015a.

2. See ch. 1 for details.

3. O'Loughlin 2016a.

4. The daylong symposium was held in the Poor Clare convent in Arkley, Barnet (UK), in spring 2016, with proceedings published in *One in Christ* 50, no. 1 (2016). The papers are Ball 2016; Cassidy 2016; Nichols 2016; Rumsey 2016; and O'Loughlin 2016b.

liturgists and theologians held in Leuven in 2017 under the auspices of the ecumenical Societas Liturgica I realized that more discussion of the topic was called for and this is the *raison d'etre* of this book. However, the aim of this book is not more theological discussion but a change in mind-set about the eucharistic *mysterium* that then manifests itself in a renewed practice.

1

Why This Book Now?

Life is greater than explanations and interpretations.
—Pope Francis, 2015

It was Christmas morning, 2018, and the church built to seat 250 people held nearly four hundred. It was a typical Christmas congregation with the regulars far outnumbered by two seasonal groups. First, there were visitors from elsewhere staying with family or friends in the area. The second contingent was those who turn up at Mass just for this feast—and there were, no doubt, several individuals who belonged to both categories. The priest was very aware of this complex mix of people and tried in the homily to say that such an infrequent appearance was okay and recalled that even such annual visits indicate a longing for God in every life. So far, welcome and inclusion were dominant themes. Then it came to the time for eating and drinking from the Lord's table and a housekeeping announcement was required about the route people should take while coming up to communion and then returning to their place. It took this form:

> For communion, there will be two stations here in the center [pointing], and there will be three people with chalices either side. So come up the center aisle, and then go back along the sides [again pointing]. If you're a non-Catholic or can't go to communion for some other reason, then remember you are very welcome to come up for a special blessing with the Blessed Sacrament, and you can show me this by crossing your arms [gesture].

There it was: the Catholic Church's position in a nutshell. Doctrine and praxis stripped free of complicated casuistry and the conditions and qualifications of canonists and ecumenical directories. It was a simple matter of black and white: if you are not a Roman Catholic, you are *not* to take communion! It was not a rule that was shouted out in an imperative *thou shalt not!* but given as a simple, factual statement as part of a practical notice intended to avoid a traffic jam. His very casualness in mentioning it showed that for that priest it was not a matter of dispute or debate. It is no more problematic than a motorist's saying one should signal before turning. Indeed, the injunction was even framed in a bizarrely positive way. You may not be able to participate in the primary goal of communion, eating and drinking, but there is a secondary commodity that is not restricted. So the friendly message was "Do not feel *too* left out, you can have a valuable consolation prize!"

I was seated off to one side and remained behind until almost the last moment, and while waiting I tried to estimate how many went up for communion and how many for a blessing. My estimate was that just under half the gathering left their seats, and, apart from small children, I saw only one adult seek a blessing. The notice clearly had been heeded, and anyone who had any doubts about eating and drinking at that Christian banquet stayed firmly where they were. Rarely is the issue of "only Catholics can go to communion" so clearly enunciated as on that Christmas morning, but the basic position is widely accepted by both Catholics and other Christians as a position set in stone. As another priest once said to me: "Them's the facts: non-Catholics are non-Catholics." Apparently, it is a simple matter, and there is no need for dispute.

A Theological Minefield

That priest's announcement about non-Catholics is neither unusual nor an extreme position identified with some specific ecclesial agenda. While there may be very nuanced positions in canon law regarding when a non-Catholic can fully share in the eucharistic meal, and this may have been given further elaboration in documents from various bishops' conferences,[1] the word on the street does not mention conscience, spiritual need, indi-

1. See Cassidy 2016 for an example of the nuanced position of a canon lawyer in comparison with the black-and-white certainties of many parish clergy.

vidual local circumstances, moral or physical impairment of access to one's own rite or ministers, or individual assent to Catholic doctrine. It simply says that only those who are explicitly Catholic (i.e., Roman Catholic) can receive. When I ask clergy, informally, if it is as clear-cut as this, the only mention of conditions takes the form that "it is different for the eastern churches," but this is very vague. Then if I ask whether it is the same for Uniate Ukrainians, Greek Orthodox, Armenians, and Copts, the answer is usually "yes" and the reason given is that "since we can take communion from them if we cannot get to [a] Mass [celebrated in the Latin Rite]," then we can reciprocate and give them communion.[2]

So, I then ask, if we can receive from a non-Catholic if that person belongs to one of the Eastern Orthodox Churches, can we go to communion in one of the local non-Catholic churches? The answer in this case is invariably a very clear "no" but with a variety of reasons offered. The reasons range from "They do not have communion" or "Receiving communion would be equivalent to accepting their theology" (and such an act of assent could not be countenanced) to the argument from validity: they do not really have the eucharist because they do not have a priest (that is, a validly ordained priest), and without a priest there is no eucharist. What about ecumenical dialogues such as *BEM*, ARCIC, and the agreements with the Lutherans?[3] These are either unknown (in the case of *BEM*), considered outdated and not having made any difference (ARCIC), or having no practical implications. The situation can only change when, in effect, all these groups are restored to complete unity with the Catholic Church, and this would, in effect, involve all their ministers being ordained (not "reordained" for they are deemed to be but laymen) as Catholic priests.

2. Needless to say, this is a very Roman Catholic-centered vision that would shock most Eastern Orthodox with its presumption that because Catholic canon law says so, such churches should meet Catholic demands! See Ware 1978 for a response to that attitude.

3. *BEM* is the document of the Faith and Order Commission of the World Council of Churches published in Lima on January 15, 1982; to appreciate it in its larger context, see Norwood 2018. ARCIC is the Anglican and Roman Catholic International Commission, which has met on and off since 1969, but after a decade of steady activity in the 1970s, it has retreated into the background and what statements it has made since the early 1980s tend to be on very abstruse points of doctrinal difference.

This position should not be dismissed as simply ignorance or confusion. The church is the people of God seeking to follow the Way, not those who have the time and inclination to keep up with the latest developments in ecumenical dialogue. The subtleties that caused so much division in the past need to be discussed with the precision of theological dialogue today, but just as the past debates produced simple, graspable (if crude) outcomes—for example, a village that had just one church in 1500 might have had two in 1600 with each side convinced that those in the other church were "lost"—so there will always be clear-cut "rules of thumb" guiding people's actions in situations like that Christmas Day Mass. Moreover, while the notion that complete unity could only come about when *every* Christian minister is ordained as a Catholic priest may seem absurd, it does fit very well with the notion that "full sacramental sharing can only occur when there is unity of belief," a statement commonly found in the documents issued by Catholic bishops' conferences on intercommunion. Perhaps this *reductio ab absurdum*—that this sort of unity will only occur at the eschaton—should point out to us that we need to think about what "unity of faith" means among Christians, and about the human timescale of everything concerning faith, discipleship, and practice.

But these are not the only problems we, as Catholics, encounter. When we discuss ecumenism we often engage in a very focused discourse, as if Catholicism is not only the center of the religious world but that all other manifestations of Christian faith are to be seen as peripheral to Catholicism. This binary self-focus, "us" and "the rest," is captured in the distinction of Catholics on one side, and then all others as "non-Catholics." Such self-focus is invariably present in human discourse, but whenever we want to engage in a dialogue that does not self-destruct on the launch pad, we need to change our approach radically. You cannot enter into a human and respectful exchange with any other individual or group if it only exists for you as being the outsiders, those who do not belong within your circle. As one goes through customs in an airport one can sort people into citizens and noncitizens. In a hospital you can divide people into patients and nonpatients, but what is a good sorting tool (dividing into *x* and *non-x*) is a flawed basis for human interaction. Would Catholics describe themselves as "non-Protestants"? What does that mean? Could you sit down and describe yourself starting from that label? Likewise, if one said one was "non-Orthodox" or a "non-Copt," one has only a tiny basis of identity, and if we are to relate to others in a respectful way—simply acknowledging our common humanity much less our common fellowship in the Lord through baptism—then we have to not only avoid the sorting mechanism but root it out of our thinking. Moreover, every positive encounter begins by a common affirmation of being parts of a commonality. In this case that could be "churches whose common identity today is founded in the division of the sixteenth century" or our common affirmation of the Nicene Creed or the more embracing reality of our common baptism.

Such a starting point is not only an acknowledgement that all human culture is full of variations—we should recall at this point that the sort of uniform consistency implicit in a world of Catholics and non-Catholics belongs more to the binary world of computer programs than that of living individuals—and that variety is the spice of life. Everyone brings something to the party. The simple fact is that Christianity has been so split by divisions, all the way back to the very start when there were Jewish Christians and Gentile Christians (and even factions within individual churches such as described in 1 Cor), that no one side in any dispute about doctrine or practice can claim to be the only way.[4] The Way is a lifestyle and an inheritance and so everyone has something to learn from the other and something to offer the other.[5]

But what does this mean for the issue of intercommunion? It is the widespread perception of every body of Christians that their theological stance is essentially simple and clear, and that complexity only relates to the outsider who sometimes must be accommodated. The problem with this assumption only becomes visible when we consider interactions between two groups of Christians. Let us examine, for instance, the assumptions at work in the statements already mentioned. Many Latin Catholics assume that because *their* authorities allow them to receive communion at Orthodox liturgies they can simply present themselves without more ado, and they then expect to be given communion. When

4. This starting point is the opposite of the myth of an early period of perfection preceding a period of decay in corruption and confusion; see Bauer 1971 for the background to the approach adopted in this book. On the persistence of myths about the early church in Christian thought, see J. Z. Smith 1990. In this book it will be assumed that complete unity and harmony is a gift of the Spirit that will only be fully realized at the End, rather than a human fact that can simply be imitated.

5. See O'Loughlin 2010, 28–45.

the Orthodox priest points out that they are not in communion and refuses their request, they are affronted![6] How could anyone, these Catholics argue, deploy such an argument against them? Surely their status as Christians could not be in doubt? This insults their own claim to be Christians. In such a situation it is easily forgotten that this is almost the same argument they deploy against other [Western] Christians. Alternatively, if those same Catholics then refuse to receive at the celebration led by an Anglican priest or a Presbyterian minister, it can come as a shock to them that this nonparticipation is not simply politely ignored—after all, they have bothered to take part by just being there!—but seen by their hosts as a theological denial of their very status as Christians. One can vary these mutual suspicions and multiply the rationales given for staying apart almost endlessly. That very fact is, to me, indicative of the flaw at the base of this whole approach to sharing in the meal of the Lord. Because the reasons vary so greatly, we are not dealing with anything that related to the eucharist as such, as an activity of Christians, but with "the eucharist" as a ritual event. It is no longer a practice but rather an indicator of group identity, a marker of the provenance of one's own group as "genuine" when in competition with some other group of Christians.

But it will be replied that there is the fact of the necessity of "valid orders" if a priest is to be a priest, and one must have a priest if one is to have a *real* eucharist, and, therefore, one is comparing a real with an unreal! While but few Catholics today would want to describe eucharistic celebrations by, for example, an Episcopalian, as a "sham"—language used until very recently—it cannot be denied that the Catholic Church insists that clergy from other denominations who become Catholic priests are ordained "absolutely"—that is, on the assumption that they have not been ordained previously. If that is a fact, and the necessity of a priest for the eucharist is a fact, then one cannot evade the next fact: they—other Western Christians—may believe sincerely that they are celebrating the eucharist, but in this they are mistaken. Such arguments are not about group identity but about "facts" that are intrinsic to the whole theological edifice. There is no way around such facts; they must simply be acknowledged in the same way that I must accept physical laws. I may need to flee from the highest floor of a burning building, but my need does not mean that I can fly!

6. Ware 1978.

This is a very serious argument not only because it is widely diffused as the theory underpinning practice but because it has a rigorous logical integrity which, when extended to its rational conclusion, arrives at the position that Catholics cannot even pray together with other Western Christians, as this would be tantamount to approving tacitly of their error. This was, indeed, the formal position of the Catholic Church until the 1960s, and it was defended as a practice by just such a logic. Moreover, I know several Orthodox priests and monks who, sincerely and logically, take that position regarding the non-Orthodox. The integrity of this position was brought home to me by three little incidents. Some years ago, I was visiting an ancient monastery in the East to look at a manuscript. The monk was most welcoming and at the end of my visit gave me a gratefully received glass of lemonade. On parting I said "Brother: let us pray for one another," and this produced a storm: he told me that Catholics had willingly engaged in a schism, had altered the creed, and so were guilty of apostasy. I was aware of this change and admitted it had taken place, therefore I was culpable and guilty, and should know the results of such apostasy. He would pray for me, but he could not do so within the liturgy nor within the church building, nor could he pray for me as a "brother." He would pray for my conversion lest I be lost forever, and so as a charity to me he would pray that I would eventually seek [a valid] baptism.

The second event was meeting an Anglican priest the day after the visit of Pope Benedict to Westminster Abbey (September 17, 2010) as we both saw a picture in a newspaper of the Archbishop of Canterbury standing alongside the pope at an ecumenical service in the abbey. My comment was "a hopeful sign of closer links." Her reply startled me: "I consider it a sham that brings the church's witness into disrepute." Her explanation was that anyone looking at it would see two brother bishops seeking to repair division, but while this might be the position of the Archbishop of Canterbury, it was not the "deep down position" of Benedict XVI. If it were the pope's position, he could still refuse to receive communion from the archbishop (on the grounds of schism) but would have to admit that the archbishop was validly ordained—and the proof would be that he would not deem Rowan Williams in need of ordination were he to become a Roman Catholic. "Actions" [in this case no second ordination], she reminded me, "count more than words!" So what should have happened when these leaders met? Her reply was that the Archbishop of Canterbury should have asked publicly: "Am I your brother bishop or a [theologically] confused layman?"

The third event was speaking to a Catholic priest ordained in the late 1950s about the changes he had lived through and asking what changes he liked and which he found difficult. He surprised me by saying that ecumenism was what he found most difficult. He had grown up saying that Protestants were heretics and were to be avoided: one was not to pray publicly with them, much less to discuss sharing the sacraments. "We knew there were things we said, and they said the opposite. We knew where we stood and where they stood. We cannot both be right!" Now he had to forget all that, forget the martyrs and all the insults they had offered to Catholic beliefs, and he was asked to call them brothers and sisters "and pretend it was all just mistakes and confusion." "If it was just that," he continued, "then, what can we trust?"

All three encounters display extreme expressions of a position, but they are valuable in drawing attention to an underlying problem. If religious reflection is a closed logical system —where all the basic truths are fully known—then continuity within the system (and that means with the past, the tradition of the system) is a supremely important test of rectitude. Moreover, there can be no change in positions that are defined as yes/no, x/not-x, valid/invalid. Theological evolution can then be no more that drawing out implications of what is already known and done, a little like watching a photograph develop. And, consequently, practice, which one should do, would be simply a spin-off from this clear and concise theological grasp of reality. However, theology is not such a closed system, nor a fully thought-out religious ideology, nor a divinely inspired game where all the rules and outcomes are known.

Christianity, rather, is primarily a matter of discipleship; it is the following of a path initiated by Jesus. As such it is a glimpse of the new way of living rather than a guidebook to a post-mortem destination. We are focused on living life, rather than the moment of death and its aftermath. Because it is a *way* of living and being together, Christianity is a commitment of love to others and God, a willingness to share with others in a tradition of worship and wisdom, and it is a moral commitment to seeking out the true and doing the good. So it is about movement, how we move, and the best way to move. Moreover, Christianity cannot be a matter that we "know it all" and our doctrine presented as "having all the answers." Instead, we are continually growing in our understanding of the implications and demands of our discipleship. Indeed, in the past we may often have been wrongheaded and embraced practices that worked not only against the grain of Christian faith but were diametrically opposed to it. So all of us might need to change and, for example, come to a new approach to ministry such that we see that we do not need to ordain, reordain, or ordain afresh those who have been ministers for years. We may need to come to a new imagining that we *all* are celebrating the eucharist when we assemble (rather than asking whether this gathering is valid, which assumes that another is not). Such change is never a simple matter, and the sort of change that this book argues for is that the default understanding of the eucharist should be that it is assumed that when Christians gather at the Lord's table they can fully share one another. Put another way, the assumption of the story with which this chapter opened was a praxis of exclusion; what we need is the opposite assumption as the basis of praxis.

That any thinking on the eucharist can be a theological minefield and draw in all sorts of other questions about ministry, priesthood, identity, and baptism has long been recognized. This is why the World Council of Churches sought to address all three issues in a single document at its Lima meeting in 1982 and its now famous statement *Baptism, Eucharist and Ministry*.[7] But whereas *BEM* sought to create a common baseline for ecumenical dialogue to help overcome centuries of strife, the aim of this book is much more modest. It wants to look at the nature of what we are doing as a community when we gather for the eucharist. Then it must see if, allowing that there are umpteen ways of explaining this (theologies), there are good reasons within the activity itself why everyone present should be presumed welcome at the table. This is a book located in the actual practice that Jesus showed us, arguing that this is a model for today, and it tries to avoid being located within the web of subsequent thinking about the activity or with the eucharist imaged as an object. "Eucharist" is the name given to a group activity, not the name of some object brought into existence by a minister. Eucharist is related to a verb, not a noun.[8]

But this approach leaves a gaping question for many people: Could it be that we really do not have all the basic truths regarding Christian faith already there and known? Is it not all there already in the Bible or in Sacred Tradition or in Scripture and Tradition? Surely, after all those centuries of argument, bitter divisions, excommunications, and even

7. See note 2 above.

8. See O'Loughlin 2015, 42.

violence toward one another in the name of faith, we cannot just say we have "moved beyond this"? This is a serious objection because, first, all the churches (but perhaps particularly the Catholic Church) have long boasted of having "all the answers," and legacy is itself an impediment to change. Second, it seems odd that a religion which claims to respond to God's revelation could simply "not see" or "get it wrong" on something central to discipleship?

There is a very interesting parallel here with Christian attitudes to slavery. Today, it is not just one church or a faction within a church that holds slavery to be an evil and incompatible with discipleship but virtually every Christian group. The notion that slavery is wrong is not found in the Bible, nor in the teaching of Jesus, nor virtually anywhere else in the mainstream Christian memory. The only group in the ancient world to condemn slavery on religious grounds—that God created each person and therefore everyone was free—were the Jews in Qumran. But Paul took slavery for granted, and down the centuries Christians owned slaves, traded slaves, and considered it the sin of theft to take someone's slaves, and these Christian slave owners went to bed with a clear conscience. When the first calls for an end to the slave trade came in the later eighteenth century, they were heard as the opinions of evangelical hotheads. Indeed, on the eve of the American Civil War a Catholic priest visiting the condemned John Brown on the night before his execution accused him of not knowing the scriptures in opposing slavery on religious grounds. Brown's reply is interesting:

> I [said the priest] remembered an epistle of St. Paul's to Philemon, where we are informed that he sent back the fugitive slave Onesimus from Rome to his master [Phm 1-6]. I then asked [Brown] what he thought of that, and he said that he did not care what St. Paul did, but what he said, and not even what he said if it was in favor of slavery![9]

The priest thought that reply settled the matter, that Brown was a religious nutcase. But what Brown had actually said was that the immediate awareness of the demands of correct practice outweighed the force of long repetition of a position. As it happened, by 1860 Catholic moral theology books were still saying that one could be a good Catholic and own slaves, but they

9. Ely and Jordan 1974.

were just beginning to question whether transporting slaves was morally permissible.[10] Those positions were never formally rejected; they just slipped into the past as people began to take it for granted that owning slaves was incompatible with discipleship, and now a rejection of slavery in every form is a standard part of Catholic Social Teaching. Here is a case where a practice that was once accepted virtually without a doubt is seen as wrong, abhorrent, and not only sinful for those directly involved in enslavement but a social evil that calls disciples to oppose it throughout the world. How did they miss something that, to us, is so blatantly obvious?

It is convenient for teachers teaching, students learning, and preachers preaching to think of revelation in terms of the conveyance of knowledge: God signals us, and we pick up the signal and acknowledge it. The nature of the conveyance might be argued about by the churches but the basic mechanism is one of information transfer, whereby we have a "download" from God among us. But this is a wholly false image. We are people of the covenant—God has established a relationship—with us and this relationship is changing and growing both with us as individuals and as groups. Like all relationships it changes, and we make new discoveries; the Spirit is constantly active showing us new wonders and leading us deeper into the divine mystery. It also goes up and down, we follow, and we wander and return, and the Spirit dwells in us prompting us toward *metanoia*. There is a constant: the constant of God's forgiving love calling us again and again to grow to the fullness of life. But the nature of the demands and the extent of our understanding of that call are always in flux. God is love, but our praxis as churches must ever be changing so that, in our changing lives, we are seeking to be more conformed to the image of God in his Christ. A change in our assumptions about our eucharistic practice need not be a betrayal of the tradition but a response to the Holy Spirit in our time.

A Pastoral Minefield

The way we view revelation seems very far from the sense of rejection I know many people felt in that church on Christmas day when the presider announced that non-Catholics were expected not to take communion.

10. Kenrick 1860, Tract 5, ch. 6 (*De servitute*), 1:164—68nn35–41.

Sharing at the Lord's table may be a point of liturgical dispute and a matter of theological debate, but it is probably the only such issue that is also—and, in my view, first and foremost—a problem for ordinary Christians as they seek to live as disciples.

The scene is one known in a myriad of homes where the partners are members of different churches, and worshipping together becomes a time of dividedness rather than celebrating their love in the presence of God. I have seen so many situations that I have tried to boil them down into a few snapshots. A couple agrees that they will go to each other's churches by turn. The Catholic says that this week it is their turn to go to Mass. The partner, not for the first time, points out that they do not like being treated as second-class citizens by being refused welcome at the table! "What is it with the Catholic Church anyway that it makes so many rules about its rituals?!" This sparks a retort: "When we go to your church there is no communion, or only the odd time, so you're not missing out. The hymns and readings are all there in both!" But, the argument gets more heated: "When my church does have communion, you don't take part: you choose to stay away!" Such simmering bitterness leads to rancor based in sincerely held positions, and there are very often casualties. A child of such a couple decides that religion only leads to argument, concluding that it should be a wholly private affair away from even those closest to you. Another child remains a Christian but believes that Christianity should give up the whole idea of Holy Communion because it only confuses and distresses people. Another common result is that rather than one partner moving to be with the other every time, both move away from church involvements: the hassle is just too much. Yet another very common result is spiritual dissonance: many churches see the eucharist as the center and summit of their worship. A few generations ago it was mainly Catholics who used this language,[11] but there has been a revolution in worship so that the table is ever more important as the focal point of Christian gathering—indeed many people see this as the Spirit's work overcoming division. But rather than the eucharist being that which brings two people together, this activity must be moved to the periphery lest it cause disharmony. Then when they hear the language of its centrality, has it any meaning for them?

11. The term is used in *Sacrosanctum concilium* 10 and in varying forms in other documents—for example, in *Eucharisticum mysterium* 1B.

Down the centuries Christians with specific needs or gifts or perspectives on discipleship have come together. Sometimes these have ended up as permanent communities, such as monasteries, sometimes as complex organizations, such as religious orders and societies, and sometimes as clubs and associations in which members work together to support one another and achieve greater results through their collaboration. Such specially focused gatherings can be seen as multipliers of the power of the Spirit. A great many such groups today even cross over the traditional denominational boundaries. Imagine a meeting of several groups of different expressions of the Franciscan charism gathered to support each other and share insights into what links them. The meeting lasts several days and involves sharing table, classroom, reflections, and relaxation—a coming together of different ways within a greater unity. The meeting draws together men and women, missionaries and teachers, contemplatives, and those engaged in a startling variety of public ministries—and it draws together Catholic and Anglican friars and sisters. One insight shared by all these groups is that we express our thankfulness through, with, and in the Christ—and so the celebration of the eucharist is a key moment in their group activity each day. Now they have come together for a few precious days of sharing and bonding, yet they split up for the eucharist. That which according to so many theologians is the center holding the church, that *catholica*, together is that which exacerbates division. Is one group really celebrating and another merely "going though the motions"? If even this way of thinking were to surface it would be destructive of mutual respect and trust; it would lead to a new tearing apart (literally: a schism) in the body of the Christ. In such situations—and they are ever more common—the times of eucharistic activity rather than being joyful and healing can be times of stress and bitterness. For centuries the Catholic Church has produced canons—all neatly gathered together—such that if someone was to hold this or that opinion about the eucharist it would be a denial of the truth and so he or she should be excommunicated. But does not that scene amount to a denial in action of a basic element of our worship that in being thankful together in the Anointed One, we are united with him, reconciled, and renewed?

The move from sectarianism (my church true; your church false) and spiritual competition (my church is better than your church) to mutual respect (we are all on the pilgrimage of faith) and support (I can learn from you; you might be able to learn from me) is one of most difficult of transitions. Old enmities, old slogans, clashing identities, our gut inclination to competition outweighing our knowledge that collaboration is more loving, and the fear of betraying the past all come into play. When we succeed in any such endeavor we are blessed. So picture a group of ministers who had succeeded in getting past ecumenical pleasantries and were now working together. Practical ecumenism had broken out. Now the next step was to share with their churches these new ways of relating to each other, and so someone suggested that they invite each other to be the guest preacher one Sunday. The benefits for all seemed obvious, but then the Catholic priest, up to that point in favor of working together, pointed out that he would have to have Mass on a Sunday and that if any other Christians came, he would have to enforce the ban on non-Catholics taking communion. The effect was like a strike of lightning! The others went ahead with the plan, but gradually the Catholics drifted away from collaboration. The Baptist minister said to me that perhaps they were too ambitious to think that they could do together "what Jesus bid them do." A minister from a charismatic church said that it seemed to him that the only way that Christians could really share was to forget the eucharist altogether: it just annoyed people. While the Catholic with sad resignation said, "What else could I do? Theology is theology." But theology does not have to be a set of instructions for a mechanism; theology is also the organized practice of Christian imagination, the means by which we move toward the vision of the world preached by Jesus.

Sharing the Lord's table is not an abstract question. How we approach it and what we do about it can have massive practical consequences for how we worship, how we relate to each other as disciples, and for the missionary witness of the church. It is an awkward issue, theologically and pastorally, that we simply must confront because, as George Lindbeck once remarked, "The eucharist tastes bitter in the divided church."[12]

A Papal Visit

When in 1983 the Western Catholic Church produced its new code of church law, it contained this very clear canon: "Catholic ministers may only lawfully administer the sacraments to the Catholic members of

12. George Lindbeck 1999.

Christ's faithful."[13] Coming hot on the heels of the Vatican's response to ARCIC, it seems that the winds favorable toward an expansive view of interaction with other Western Christians had now turned very wintry. This more negative attitude to anything that hinted at discussion of eucharistic sharing fitted the mood emanating from the Congregation of the Doctrine of the Faith under Cardinal Josef Ratzinger (later Pope Benedict XVI). This new tone—that change could only come when *de facto* there was complete ecclesial union—was set out afresh in the document *One Bread One Body*, produced by the bishops in the British Isles but taken as an expression of the official line far more widely. Among many Catholic theologians there was a belief that this was no longer an open question, and certainly it was one that many theologians in church employment believed was too fraught for discussion. Meanwhile, many theologians in other churches believed that, sadly, it was a futile question to pursue as no real progress was possible. Indeed, it seemed to Protestant observers—as with the new English text of the sacramentary in 2011—that the Catholic Church was doing all it could to put as much clear blue water between itself and the other Western churches.[14] Paradoxically, in the same decades when Catholic officials were withdrawing from eucharistic debate, there was a massive upsurge in ecumenism—beginning in the pews with Catholics joining in the eucharistic meals of others and inviting others to join them at their tables. Equally paradoxically, those decades have seen an interest in the eucharist growing among Protestant churches, from across the spectrum, that is unparalleled since the 1550s. But if anyone were asked to describe in one word the situation between those churches and the Catholic Church in the early twenty-first century, that would probably have been "impasse."

Then on Sunday, November 15, 2015, Pope Francis paid a visit to a Lutheran church in Rome as part of the celebrations of "Lutherjahr"—five hundred years since Luther published his famous Ninety-Five Theses on October 31, 1517. Part of that visit was a discussion between the pope and members of that community, and he was asked questions by a child and two women. One of these women, Anke de Bernardinis, asked this question:

13. Canon 844.1.

14. Bradshaw 2014.

> Like many persons of our community, I'm married to an Italian who is a Roman Catholic Christian. We have been living happily together for many years, sharing joys and sorrows. And, therefore, it's quite painful to be divided in the faith and to be unable to take part together in the Lord's Supper. What can we do on this point to finally attain communion?[15]

Here was the nub of the question—not framed as an abstract puzzle but as an actual problem for two Christians on their pilgrimage of life and faith. The pope gave quite a lengthy reply, but what is most interesting is that instead of a fixed answer he gave some starting points *toward* an answer. He began by noting that the Christian journey began with the Last Supper in Jerusalem and will end with the last Last Supper—the banquet of the kingdom—in the New Jerusalem. So there we have a eucharistic Alpha moment and an Omega point, but then the pope wondered whether in the intervening period—our human now when we are on the journey of faith—we may have to think in terms of means and not ends. The pope said:

> Instead on the journey, I wonder—and I don't know how to answer, but I make your question my own—I wonder: Is the sharing of the Lord's Supper *the end* of a journey or the *viaticum* to journey together? I leave the question to the theologians, to those who understand.

The most notable aspect of this is that, whatever answer is given to Anke's question, this is a question, a real question, and one which needs to be explored. At a stroke, the comments of so many bishops and theologians over a period of more than a quarter of a century that this was a closed question were set aside. Moreover, by distinguishing what we do in our temporal fractured existence—the time of journey, pilgrimage, living, and of sacraments—from the final times of the church in the heavenly kingdom Pope Francis pinpointed the weakness of so many discussions of the question which, starting from the eschaton, could not move from perfection to the imperfection of human living, and then found that they argued in a closed circle. The pope moved the issue from a discussion of finalities, final purposes, that is characteristic of a certain neoscholastic

15. For the complete account of the pope's visit, see https://zenit.org/articles/pope-s-visit-to-lutheran-community-in-rome/.

approach to theology[16] to a discussion based on the idea that the eucharist is "food for a journey" (*viaticum*) and so belongs to the world of where we are now.[17] If we think in terms of *viaticum* rather than ends, we have to ask what we are doing when we engage as disciples and how our actions help other disciples on their journey. This shift from the eschaton to discipleship in the pope's way of thinking is an invitation to Catholics to imagine the eucharist in a rather unfamiliar way. The key question is now: How would intercommunion help all of us as we live our lives?

This new stance is then addressed in a slightly different way when the pope says: "Don't we have the same Baptism? And if we have the same Baptism, we must walk together." Again his approach is based on discipleship and the image of Christian living as walking—and walking *together*. The various churches are not to be imagined as one being "on the tracks" and the others not moving, but that we are all embarked on this journey: we walk together. And this pilgrimage is not accidental but is founded in a genuine belonging to a single community through baptism. Having the same baptism means we are all members of the one church—the *catholica* we affirm in the creeds—before we are in churches with one doctrine or another. We are part of the one baptismal church

16. There is a scholastic maxim that "whatever acts acts in view of an end," and this approach underpins much theological thinking that sees *purpose* and *the end* and *finality* as intertwined and intimately linked with the nature of an object or activity. But while this is a useful rule of thumb in dealing with everyday matters (asking "What is a car for?" is a good way of understanding the nature of an automobile), it is limited in theological enquiry precisely because we cannot know the eschaton in the way we understand finite reality. What we will be in the kingdom is a mystery—and sacraments are *mysteries* precisely because they somehow stand between our imperfectly grasped now, our imperfect lives, and a future that is only grasped now "in shadows and images" (John Henry Newman). Anyone addressing any question relating to sacraments using a scholastic framework should reflect on Paul's "For now we see in a mirror, dimly, but then we will see face to face. Now I know only in part; then I will know fully, even as I have been fully known. And now faith, hope, and love abide, these three; and the greatest of these is love" (1 Cor 13:12-13).

17. *Viaticum* means, literally, one's traveling money, and it has developed the meaning of "food for a journey" in relation to communion at the moment of death—it was for this purpose that eucharistic reservation emerged within the Western church. The key image is that the eucharist, as a sacrament, belongs to the pilgrim, moving along life's way, situation: this will be examined in detail in chapter 7 of this book.

before we are members of churches with their own languages and approaches, and this led the pope to reflect on the family as its own church with its own ecclesial integrity.

It is this reality of discipleship, of our real belonging to the one church through baptism, and the integrity of the actual Christian situations we find ourselves in that prompts the pope to distinguish between the reality of our lives, on the one hand, and the various explanations and interpretations—what we might call abstract theological reflection—on the other. In our lives we deal with realities, upon which we reflect, but it is all too easy to start with our abstractions and then seek to fashion reality upon our interpretations. In Pope Francis's words: "Life is greater than explanations and interpretations. Always make reference to Baptism: 'One faith, one Baptism, one Lord,' so Paul says to us, and from there take the consequences."

The pope's clear answer was that a pastoral and practical solution is called for given that it is a practical situation, but also that this is something that should be explored by theologians. So this book is an attempt to take up that papal request. However, it is not simply a case that theologians must come up with a theoretical justification for intercommunion, but, given such statements as that of the presider on Christmas Day 2018, they must also create a new pastoral vision. In this vision, the idea that someone should place their "non-Catholicism" in doctrine over their Catholicism in baptism has to become practically unthinkable.

An Approach from Practice

In trying to tease out a practical vision that follows on in spirit, theme, and tone from the reply of one Christian, Pope Francis, to another, Anke de Bernardinis, the difficulty is to avoid working with abstract generalizations while at the same time producing a vision that applies more widely than an individual situation. My way through this tension is to focus on the actual realities of what we do when we assemble for the eucharist. So the justification for intercommunion should be seen to come of the actuality of the eucharist itself. We act as communities of sisters and brothers when we gather at the Lord's table, so it should be the nature of what we are doing there that determines who can and cannot be around that table.

This approach, of its nature, cannot have the tight coherence of pursuing a body of evidence all leading to a single point. Rather, in each of the following chapters there will be one way of looking at intercommunion that can stand or fall on its own merits. Each is a pointer toward a direction of travel. My aim is to show that it is incompatible with who we are and what we are doing to take part in a eucharist and, then, not wish all present to share fully in the Lord's Supper at which they are companions—and companions at a table eat and drink together. For the time being, we live in a world of signs and pointers, understanding in part, and full understanding belongs to the kingdom, and our priority is moving forward in love.[18]

18. See 1 Cor 13:12-13.

2

The Grammar of Meals

Manners Maketh Man.
—motto of New College, Oxford

Some Basic Facts

An ever-increasingly connected planet has taught us that the number of universally valid statements we can make about humanity is very small. The hoary old example of such a statement from logic textbooks, "All human beings are mortal," is still undisputed, but the confidence of earlier generations that they could say "All human are . . ." or "All human beings desire . . ." has been shaken by our awareness of how cultures vary, their values mutating over time, and the untold complexity of humans that has been revealed by psychology. That said, we can make some assertions. First, in the last few hours (or in the next few hours) you, the reader, will consume liquid: water or some other liquid with a high proportion of water such as coffee, tea, milk, cola, whatever. All human beings need water for hydration to live. This cannot be disputed, and if you have not drunk water in the last few hours or in the next few hours, or received liquid in some other form (by intravenous drip, for example), then you would be better off sourcing hydration than reading this book. Second, in the last day or so (or today or tomorrow), you will have consumed sustenance: we need to eat, fairly regularly, if we are to survive. "Humans need food to live" is another universal proposition. Again, this need has a priority in our existence: we eat or we die, and it is a fact about our lives we simply cannot change at will.

Now we can move to less certain matters. It is likely that when you next eat, and slightly less so with regard to drinking, you will do this in company. You will eat the food you need as part of a joint endeavor with your partner, your family, or some other group of people. You may welcome such company—a word that comes from "companion," meaning "someone you share bread with"—or you may prefer to eat and drink alone. Such individual preferences destroy the possibility of saying "All humans eat in groups." However, humans as a group not only often eat together but they see this as something desirable and pleasurable. So, for example, we often have dining rooms in our houses, in common buildings there will be places where common eating can take place, and you cannot travel along many streets before you see a restaurant, coffee shop, or some source of fast food or street food. Even if you forego all such occasions for eating with other human beings, however, virtually all the food we eat presupposes a human network.[1] Clearly this is the case with processed food, and all the products of agriculture (cereals, for example), and most food needs a logistic network to store and deliver it to us when we need it, but even the simplest hunter-gatherer society assumes that obtaining food is a collective activity. When we humans nourish ourselves, we do it as part of a community.

But if eating and drinking and our survival is always a communal affair, it is also a social affair—that is, it relates to us not just as consuming animals but as creative centers of consciousness. As an animal species we have spent more time down the millennia in the pursuit of foodstuff than any other activity, but having spent all that effort hunting, gathering, and producing food, we then expend even more effort in order to cook and prepare that foodstuff before we actually eat it. So now we come to another universal statement: humans are the only animals who cook their food. And, once again, this can happen only through complex human cooperation: one person can sow and reap, another can mill, another organizes the oven (whether the cooking involves gathering wood for a fire or simply flicking an electric switch, in every case there is the presupposition of a human network), another bakes the bread, and several eat it. Food—much more than the raw foodstuff—links us together and makes us a society. We can go further, for we eat not just regularly as our bodies

1. In fact, the exceptions (such as finding edible berries or mushrooms by accident as one walks) are anomalies (and risky).

require but we eat as a society.[2] At a simple level we know cultures vary in the number and times of meals each day, and at a more complex level we know that cultures have moments of eating together to mark off the significant events of living. But even if many animals eat together (hunting animals around prey is an example), we do so out of deliberate choice. So we arrive at another universal: we are the only animals who share meals. We prepare our food for sharing with one another, and the coming together to eat it is much more than the practicality of saving effort through joint enterprise. Sharing meals, which is far more than sharing food, is profoundly *and uniquely* human.

And so yet another universal: human society is built up by sharing meals. We are banqueting animals. The great wedding festival, traditionally marking not only an event for two people but, more importantly, two family groups, is a case in point. That feast is not just a big meal—indeed, in terms of acquiring food it is unnecessary—but a most profound moment in the life of a community. Almost every human event, in fact, is marked with shared meals. From the child's birthday party to the shared meals of adventurous adolescents—and it is not important whether it is popcorn and cola or burgers and beer—we mark such occasions with shared meals. And as we grow toward maturity, with the intimate shared meals of young couples, wedding feasts, retirement dinners, and funeral meals, we mark our lives with shared meals. Shakespeare can have Hamlet cry

> Thrift, thrift, Horatio! The funeral's baked meats
> Did coldly furnish forth the marriage tables[3]

and be sure that an audience will know that there is something tragic afoot. John can have Jesus do "the first of his signs" at a wedding in Cana and be equally sure that his audience understands this is a significant event (John 2).[4]

2. Goody 1998 is a good exploration of this theme; for the anthropological background, see Jones 2007 for a brilliant account of how sharing food has been a central theme of human development.

3. Shakespeare, *Hamlet*, act 1, sc. 2.

4. The biblical examples in this chapter are not to be understood as in some way "proof texts" or as authorities; they are simply illustrations well known to a theological reader that meal sharing is central to human culture, and that an appeal to the assumptions about meals—that is, their grammar—is not alien to theological discourse.

Meals mean much to us humans. And so we come to a final universal: humans as social animals are bonded to each other through shared meals. Whenever we forget this basic human truth in anything we say or do regarding the eucharist—an activity whose basic actions are eating and drinking together as a community—we end up with producing religious-sounding nonsense.

Meals Have Structure

How we share meals varies. In one culture it may be customary for all the men to eat in one house, while the women eat in another. In some places the main meal of the day is around noon; elsewhere it is in the evening. Some places have a special interest in particular meals that are more than special: Thanksgiving in the United States and Canada is a good example, while in Britain, despite very few people noting Sunday by any form of religious observance, there is still a big market for "Sunday Lunch." Some meals can only be shared by special groups—the members of college, a monastic order, or an officers' mess—while others are relatively open, but whether the group is closed or open all know some implicit rules of how the sharing takes place. We have implicit assumptions, unwritten rules about how we participate in various kinds of meals. It is a group activity, and we simply *know* how to do it.

These implicit assumptions tell us about ourselves as a society and about how we relate to one another. Indeed, the constant presence of such assumptions means that no common meal is without some structure that is known and accepted, mostly unconsciously, by each participant. Anyone who does not know these rules or cannot cope with them is immediately reminded that this is not how we do things! If human society is intimately related to sharing meals, then human and humane culture depends on our shared table assumptions. The three-word alliterative motto of New College captures this insight: "Manners Maketh Man." It is what we assume about our interactions with one another, so often in the sharing of meals, that creates a distinctly human society rather than a pack of the same species of animal. We might be more precise: "Table manners make us human." But mention of table manners brings back bad memories of being five-year-olds told how to hold a knife properly, and, consequently, we treat the idea as silly. But we all have the table manners that allow us to fit into the meals we are actually sharing. This has led anthropologists to speak of "the grammar of meals."[5] Just as our human sharing of language has an implicit structure (a grammar) that allows us to attain, however roughly, common understanding, so our meal-sharing supposes common structures that allow us to have the meal together and to find it a humanly satisfying experience.

Anthropologists, sociologists, and historians of culture can go into exquisite detail on these grammars—there are more grammars of meals than there are grammars of languages—and their significance.[6] Here we can simply note two points. First, the existence of these grammars is a fact. This can be easily demonstrated: go into any diner, or pub serving food, and the "main meal" menu will come first, then the sweet, dessert, or pudding list. Everyone expects that people will eat lasagne before they eat ice cream—and a departure from that sequence will cause surprise. Second, these manners are not simply arbitrary, made up on the spot, but are there before we begin our meal. We accept them and this acceptance is part of our culture, part of who we are.

The Elements of the Grammar

Whether or not there are universal elements within this grammar of meals—the equivalent of stating that every language has a mixture of nouns and verbs—can be a matter of dispute. I suspect that there are some elements of the grammar of meal-sharing that are as universal as the fact that humans are meal-sharing animals, but pursuing this question here would be a distraction. Rather we should note that there are some elements that are known to most people whose cultural origins (like that of Judaism, Christianity, and Islam) lie in the urban Mediterranean world. We think of meals as taking place at a table, and the notion of having a place at a table is very much part of welcoming, being welcome, and belonging. This can be experienced when, for example, there are two tiers of wedding invitations and the smaller, closer group is invited to the whole feast, while a wider group is invited to just a part of it. Such split invitations are fraught with danger: there will always be some who believe they should be in the first rather than the second group—and so will be

5. The basic work is Douglas 1972; Mary Douglas appears to have been the first scholar who used the analogy of grammar for our implicit meal assumption.

6. For a brilliant survey, see Visser 1993.

insulted and hurt. Strangely, while I have heard people say they were surprised to be in the first group, I have never heard of anyone saying they should be moved or relegated to the second tier. This same assumption underlies Luke's teaching when he has Jesus give this piece of discipleship wisdom:

> When he noticed how the guests chose the places of honor, he told them a parable. "When you are invited by someone to a wedding banquet, do not sit down at the place of honor, in case someone more distinguished than you has been invited by your host; and the host who invited both of you may come and say to you, 'Give this person your place,' and then in disgrace you would start to take the lowest place. But when you are invited, go and sit down at the lowest place, so that when your host comes, he may say to you, 'Friend, move up higher'; then you will be honored in the presence of all who sit at the table with you. For all who exalt themselves will be humbled, and those who humble themselves will be exalted." (Luke 14:7-11)

The grammar of meals is assumed, and Luke can use it as the paradigm for Christian humility.

Tables are places of welcome, and once there, we see ourselves as belonging and we expect others to see us as belonging. We get a very interesting example of this element of the grammar of meals in the gospels. Luke has Jesus stay with the outcast Zacchaeus, sharing his hospitality, and this is scandalous for the grumblers who say, "He has gone to be the guest of one who is a sinner" (Luke 19:7). This tale only works as a proclamation of the gospel if among the audience, the grumblers they hear about, and Zacchaeus and Jesus there is a common assumption about welcome, having a place at table, and what that says about our humanity.

Another assumption about hospitality is that what we have available we share, and we share with those who are with us. If I am present in your house at a mealtime, then basic courtesy demands that you invite me to eat with you. Likewise, I cannot *not* welcome you to my table if you are present and I am about to sit down and eat. In a purely functional, contractual relationship where I am seeking a service from you, or vice versa, it is not expected that we would eat together, but if this is a relationship of friends it would be strange if we did not have a common table. Moreover, such a welcome to the table is part of traditional hospitality, and the refusal of hospitality is interpreted as enmity. Indeed, mealtimes set up a strange dynamic within any relationship because good manners demand that I do not exclude you, but likewise good manners demand that you do not refuse to eat with me. Put another way, if either positively refuses to share a meal that could be shared, then that refusal is a very significant indicator about how one views the other. Being present, in effect, demands both welcoming and acceptance: here is a key part of the human grammar of meals. Again, we have an interesting example of this assumption in Paul: "If an unbeliever invites you to a meal and you are disposed to go, eat whatever is set before you without raising any question on the ground of conscience" (1 Cor 10:27). Paul assumes the basic element of the grammar: if you have agreed to be present at a meal, then you share in it—and good manners further demand that you do not "make a fuss."

Assuming that the other, the stranger, is made welcome—and is there anything so heartwarming for the stranger than this—then another grammatical rule comes into play. The stranger gets the better portion! You make sure that the stranger, now your guest, is put at ease and courtesy gives the guest priority. This expresses itself in many little ways. When there is not enough to go around for both family and guests, there is often a little coded message that the family hold back so that the guests do not go short. If a guest's glass is empty one thinks of filling it before one's own; or if there is only one piece of pie left, then the visitors have first call upon it. There is a lovely story of a banquet given by King Edward VII when a foreign visitor drank the water in the fingerbowl, and then, when some others at the table sniggered, the king took up his bowl and drank its contents. The guest must not feel excluded, or an unwritten boundary in decent human conduct has been crossed. This element of the grammar of meals, that the visitor must experience the fullness of welcome, is an assumption in any number of stories. Without this assumption the welcoming meal by Abraham for the three strangers (Gen 18:1-16) when he had cakes of "fine flour" and "a good and tender calf" and "curds and milk" set before them as a meal makes little sense. We now often see an icon of this story, such as that by Andrei Rublev, and call it "the icon of the Trinity," but in reflecting on the Trinity we should not bypass the icon's immediate story: it is our father Abraham welcoming the strangers by sharing his best food with them.[7] Moreover, it is this story of sharing

7. Hence this icon's title in Greek, "The *Xenodochium* of Abraham," which we could render as "When Abraham Ran a Guesthouse."

food with strangers that forms the basis, for whoever wrote the letter to the Hebrews, of the Christian practice of hospitality to strangers: "Let mutual love continue. Do not neglect to show hospitality to strangers, for by doing that some have entertained angels without knowing it" (Heb 13:1-2). Likewise, for Luke, the same assumption underpins his story of the father's feast at the return of his lost son: the one who has been outside is welcomed inside by being given the finest fare for his feast (Luke 15:11-32).

The understanding that shared food is at the base of proper human behavior is so widespread that the very thought of it not happening is tantamount to a dystopia. Hell is where each feeds herself and himself rather than neighbors serving one another. When each is fearful that the other will steal from you, rather than share with you, then true human life has broken down: in such situations we have ceased to be human animals. A world where people refuse to share food with "the other" is on the way toward being a cesspool of nastiness; it is the antithesis of the world for which Christians work, and it is the opposite of Christian hope expressed as looking toward the Lord's banquet.

The Grammar of Meals and the Meal of Meals

If the central act of Christian worship were something like the daily sacrifices of the Second Temple—burnt offerings morning and evening—or like the worship performed in most of the temples across the Greco-Roman world, then all the regulations of that liturgy could be proclaimed as coming from some authoritative text or some oracular source. We could just make them up, and the more bizarre the better: they would have the feel of "otherness" of so much human religious experience. But the central ritual action of Christian discipleship takes the form of a meal: we gather around a table to eat and drink. Like it or not (and down the centuries countless Christians have *not* liked it and done everything possible to minimize this fact of a meal), the given, the datum, the basic fact is that we see ourselves fulfilling a command of the Lord that we eat and drink together (see 1 Cor 11:23). As such, this central act of faith is also a human act—for it to be the most significant meal means it must be already a meal—and so all that is inherent in human meal-sharing is also inherent to this liturgy. We just cannot ignore it without either ignoring our humanity or the Lord's command. Part of the structure of our liturgy is laid down in our humanity, long before we develop custom, codify rubrics, promulgate canons, or produce theological deductions. The core of the grammar of meals is not something we can just make up or change to suit us; it is hardwired into us as humans. This grammar cannot simply be set aside because of some other concern without us betraying the very structure, a meal, that was the choice of the Lord Jesus for his followers. Before we can even start thinking about the meal theologically, we must respect the human values that are inherent in every meal.

This means that if I am willing to let someone be present at the meal, I cannot refuse a guest a share in all that I have. Likewise, that visitor cannot accept my hospitality by being present and then refuse to share food with me. Meal-sharing sets up a complex web of mutual interaction. What does this mean in practice?

If I am the presider, and so acting as the host at the table, then I must make everyone present welcome and ensure that those who might see themselves as strangers or visitors know that this is a place of human sharing. Good human manners means that I must assume everyone present will want to eat and drink at the table. I have not stopped them coming into the meal, so now, by virtue of the grammar of meals, I cannot refuse to let them eat. If I am one of those at the meal and see it as a meal of my church, then I should be watchful for the guests and help them feel welcome. This is obvious when one sees those who do not know their way around our hymnbook or service sheet and one helps them "find their place," but it should extend to helping them see that what we have we share. No one should depart from our liturgy having felt that eating and drinking was only for the insiders; we have all become insiders to one another because we are companions in a meal.

So what does it mean if I see myself as a guest, a visitor, at the eucharist? It means that I should behave properly at the meal: this is not the place for staging a theological protest that attacks the underlying human structure upon which the Lord established the liturgy. If I want to stage a theological protest or someone wants to stage one at our eucharist, then it should be done elsewhere: once you have arrived at the liturgy it is too late, for having "come in" one must behave properly. It means that if I am present at a eucharist celebrated by, for example, a community of Episcopalians, I respect the grammar of that meal and share, since I am welcome, in its food and drink. And rejoicing in that sharing I am thankful to God for this welcome and this reminder that we shall all one day sit at his table when "many will come from east and west and will eat with Abraham and Isaac and Jacob in the kingdom of heaven" (Matt 8:11).

But what if those who are present see themselves as lawfully present in that they are Catholics but are excluded from communion? We have a long history of this attitude to the eucharist thinking in terms of the sharing by those who are "worthy."[8] This rule, and other purity regulations of one sort or another, has meant that the majority of Christians, for the greater part of Christian history, have not shared in the eating and drinking that is at the heart of the event.[9] Sharing in the meal is not a reward for good behavior, and we cannot use the refusal of hospitality as penalty without destroying the very basis of Christian love. We are all incomplete, we are all sinners, we are all on a journey, and it is precisely as such that the Lord welcomes us to his meal—just as he often was criticized for eating and drinking with sinners before this. So as participants in the meal we eat and drink thankful that it is the Father's hospitality rather than our incompetence that has the last word.

It also implies that we have a certain integrity of action surrounding the eucharist. If I am *not* going to share the food and drink of this meal with you, I should make that abundantly clear beforehand: "Do not come to my meal!" I should list those who are welcome and those who are not. This way I would maintain the human dignity of my actions: I am not such a host as would welcome strangers. But once one expresses this idea in this way, one sees it is incompatible with our understanding of a loving God from whom no one is a stranger and who rejoices in the return of the outcast. Moreover, as the Jansenists found, once one starts excluding those who are not welcome, one quickly must extend the list: it might be the Protestants and the divorced-and-remarried today, tomorrow it will be those who do not accept a particular formula enshrined in Denzinger and those who fail in discipleship in some other way, and eventually the list will exclude you—and me.[10]

8. The origins of this thinking are often seen to lie in 1 Cor 11:27; but reading Paul shows this is not a basis for excommunication but an enjoinder to celebrate the meal together without the divisions that so worried Paul (see 11:17).

9. See ch. 7 below, where this will be examined in more detail.

10. See Knox 1950, 176–230, for a lucid account of how the book of Jansenist theologian Antoine Arnault (1612–94), *Fréquent Communion*, written to encourage more frequent communion, "held its unlovely sway" (229) to the effect of making communion even *less* frequent than it had been in the later medieval and Renaissance periods—and its effects were still being felt in Catholicism, well beyond the visible bounds of Jansenism, until the mid-twentieth century.

But Can We Treat the Eucharist as a Meal?

It may seem a mighty jump from anthropology to eucharistic sharing, and an even greater jump to saying that one should not refuse people just on the basis of manners. Let us consider these situations. Until the early 1960s there was rarely a situation where anyone who was not a Catholic would ever have found themselves at a Mass and even considered taking communion. Attendance at a Mass was part of the "superstition" or "works-righteousness" of Catholics, and it was very clear that this was the very disease from which the churches of the Reformation were fleeing. Such a person would not have wanted to be associated with this Romish "hocus pocus" and might have learned as a child to deride it with such a song as the "Hokey Pokey." Thankfully, such bitter barrier building between Christians is passing. Moreover, the question of hospitality hardly arose because as recently as the early 1960s the fasting rules and the dregs of Jansenism meant that very few Catholics went to communion. The old notion that you had to go once a year was interpreted to mean that so long as that was done, anything more was only for the zealous. Mass and communion were seen as separate events, and there was very little chance that any Catholic ever thought about communion as a meal: even phrases like "the Lord's Supper," which could point out the meal form of the event, were unknown among Catholics.

Today we have a liturgy that brings out in words and actions the meal dimension of offering thanks to the Father in the manner of Jesus, and so once again we know we are engaging in a human act that is an encounter with the divine mystery. It is our sacramental meal, but the human basis of this *sacramentum*, this *mysterium*, is a meal—and as a meal it participates in the whole human reality of meals. "But," bellowed an irate Catholic priest to me, "the Holy Sacrifice is much more than a matter of human 'manners'!" Yes, it is much more, but it is still a matter of human manners unless we all stop sharing food and drink at our eucharistic celebrations. It is true that many Catholic preachers have seen a clash between the vertical and the horizontal dimensions of liturgy and thereby minimized the latter, and some have gone even further and argued that to emphasize the vertical dimension we must play down the meal aspect arguing that it is "a mere form" or "a sacred meal" that is *sui generis*. The meal is not simply a framework for something else,[11] but a reality within

11. Compare Ratzinger 2000, 78.

our human world that is also a mystery embracing the divine. One can do this, but a meal is a meal—and if this particular meal is *sui generis*, a wholly unique event in our experience, then it loses its sacramental connection with the whole of life and creation. And if we do go down that route—as we have done accidentally in the past—then let us acknowledge that we would then be operating outside of the memory of the actions of Jesus and his meals.

So we can say that:

- Every meal has a grammar that is antecedent to any interpretation we place upon it.
- In being a meal, the eucharist cannot but have this grammar operating within as a human reality.
- Hospitality is part of the best of our humanity and expresses itself in our sharing of meals.
- We cannot refuse to share with anyone present with us without damaging the very humanity that is the basis of our Christian dignity.
- We cannot be present at the meal and unwilling to eat and drink, for this is part of what it means to be there at this human event.
- If we betray the human reality, we vitiate the basis of the sacramental reality.
- If we suspect valuing what is truly human and noble in our humanity—sharing our table with strangers and creating a culture of peace and welcome—then we may find that we are not placing a high enough value on the central moment in Christian history when the Word became one of us.

3

Pray My Sisters and Brothers

That the dining table is one of the best places for communication—perhaps the ideal place, where the desire to communicate with one's familiars is expressed with ease and freedom—is so evident and so readily observable in daily life that there is no need for historical confirmation.
—Massimo Montinari[1]

In the last chapter I tried to look at what we are doing as human beings when we share meals, and I argued that the intrinsic nature of this activity determines the parameters of what is acceptable behavior when we celebrate the eucharist. One aspect of human meal-sharing is that if a stranger comes into our community we make the guest welcome through sharing our meal. Conversely, a refusal to eat together, whether that comes from the host or the guest, sets up or entrenches a boundary between people, deepens division, and pushes us toward increased mutual antagonism. But is that scenario of making the stranger welcome an adequate way to view the presence of some fellow Christian at our eucharistic gathering? Is a fellow Christian really an outsider?

Siblings in the Christ

There are very few eucharistic assemblies in the Catholic Church today where anyone, even the presider, knows everyone. The presider might

1. Montinari 2015, 177.

know everyone by sight, but I doubt if he could name everyone. Moreover, as dioceses adapt to having fewer presbyters, the number of people at each Sunday eucharist tends to get steadily larger. So there is a real sense in which every gathering is a meeting of strangers. And, if such is the nature of our meeting then perhaps worrying about strangers is silly: who cares so long as all get Mass and as many as are willing to go up for communion can get it.[2] However, this viewpoint is derived from a diseased state of the liturgy and one that has forgotten that a meal where we share a loaf and a cup is not something that can be just "scaled up." The nature of our gathering is as a community where we affirm that as sisters and brothers we will travel the way of discipleship together. By its nature this is a small-scale affair. In this setting we need to remind ourselves that each of us is called by name within the church and so in any assembly of the church we should know the members of our local community as individuals. If we celebrate the eucharist within a situation where we only know the names of our immediate family, then we can only say by a very stretched metaphor that we are a community of sisters and brothers who bear witness as a church in that place. In such "scaled up" situations Christianity has, in effect, been replaced by a religious individualism. But we should note that this situation of liturgical anonymity is both relatively new and is perverse. The early churches met in domestic spaces—and so there were many churches each with a few people. Medieval Christians met in village churches and these were as numerous as those villages, and even in cities there were umpteen small churches catering for smaller localities within the city. It is only in recent centuries when the size of congregations is a direct function of the number of ministers that the anonymous (either wholly or in part) has made its ugly appearance. So let us think in terms of communities where we know each other, can call upon one another by the name given us when we entered the church at baptism, and where we have a sense that we, all of us, are the people of God who bear witness to the truth of the gospel as a community. This may be far from where you are now, but no other starting point is worthy of us who are called to be the church through the Father's love.

2. We Catholics must be continually aware of how our habitual language leads us astray in treating the eucharist as an object in a world of religious objects and indeed, allowing for its sacramental nature, as an object with extension in the natural world.

But this gathering is at once both intimate and open. It is intimate in that we have a sense of our being a community, calling each other by our *Christian* name, but it is also open because others can join us—indeed, we openly welcome visitors. Moreover, we know that we are one church, but also that we are part of a whole worldwide network of churches. We could even say that the Christian church is one of the first groups who could adopt the motto: "Think global, act local."[3] The assumption of the network of churches that forms the *oikoumene* is that any other member of the church is welcome: we will find space, and we will find them a place at our table. So I am simultaneously a member of this church—a very visible network of people gathered in one place today—and of the church that is an international network that keeps in touch with its churches, just as the first churches kept in touch with one another sharing skills, and resources, and people, and letters.[4] Indeed, I should have a sense that if I turn up at any church I will be brought in and the people there will address me as their brother. This is the very heart of what *catholicism*—as a fact about the Christian gathering that we confess in the creed—means. It was this catholicism, that every disciple of Jesus is a sister or brother, that underpinned the collection for the famine in Syria that we hear about in 2 Corinthians. Likewise, it underpins the movements of Paul around the Mediterranean, the great motif of the latter part of the Acts of the Apostles. Without this sense of network, we would not have four gospels accepted as canonical in every one of the churches. So, if another follower of Jesus is a sister or brother, just from outside our local group, to what extent can that person be a stranger? That person may on arrival be unknown by name, but that is very different from that sister or brother being an alien, an outsider, an "other."

Sadly, between the *catholicism* so many Christians confess and the actual networks of churches we have the phenomenon of division. We have networks of churches, denominations, that do not see communion as extending to other networks and who express their identity by breaking communion, *excommunicating* each other. And on the other hand we have endeavors to preserve communion—activities like the ministry of the patriarchs, the Petrine ministry, the Synod of Bishops, and the Lambeth Conference—which try to ensure that the tendency of human beings to

3. O'Loughlin 2010, 105–12.

4. Thompson 1998.

split off into factions is counteracted. We also have endeavors like the World Council of Churches, whose work is to patch up communion this way and that between these networks (its agenda is found in its one-word motto, *oikoumene*), and its various formal meetings to try to resolve differences on doctrine. Likewise, at the local level we have conflicting evidence. On the one hand, we have the tendency to identify difference as a betrayal of the gospel, and so a different group must be named and rejected. And there are also those who believe and feel that they can no longer associate with others because of what they preach or do, and so want to form a fresh distinct community. On the other hand, however, the local level also sees people forging bonds between groups and working across their differences in the name of the gospel. It is worth examining these two tendencies—toward ecumenism and toward sectarianism—in greater detail, for the fact that these phenomena exist side by side is of great importance for intercommunion.

For most Christians the history of division is very simple. There was the faith "once for all delivered to the saints" (Jude 3) and proclaimed by the apostles, who "devoted themselves to . . . teaching and fellowship" (Acts 2:42), and all was well within the church. Then corruption set in, greed and false teaching caused division, and this destruction had to be rejected. Thus difference was always a "tearing" (*schisma*) of something that was one and whole, while a "sect" (*haeresis*) was something that is in opposition to the rest. But built into both concepts is not only a romantic view of origins but an assumption that Christian faith is a fixed body of structured and consistent doctrine that was downloaded by the apostles (who, incidentally, were also a highly organized and harmonious group operating at the same time such that each statement of Paul fitted with each of the evangelists). This myth of original consistency and unity is emotionally attractive, seems to be logically consistent with the notion that there is an authoritative Christian doctrine, and it is one that is relatively easy to preach. In short, there was God-given unity at the alpha-point and subsequently human-made division—and unity is the challenge of those who have departed, who must now recognize their failures in thoughts or deeds and return to the fold.

But the history of the Christian movement is rather more complex. A good place to start is with Paul writing to the Corinthians urging them to accept the differences between hands and feet while knowing that every body has many parts—and it is when all the parts work together that there is the one body of the Christ (1 Cor 12). For Paul, unity and consistency are not a past reality but a potential within us that we must seek to bring to perfection. There are divisions, differences, but these must be overcome so that the glory of the Christ will be revealed. Unity, all working together with the harmony and accord of foot, hand, and eye within the healthy body of the skilled worker, is a future reality, an Omega-point, toward which we travel with the Spirit's guidance. This theological vision of unity as a destination fits with everything we see from the historical study of Christian origins, for we find anything but the consistency and organization that is implicit in the alpha-point model. The followers of Jesus came from different sects within Judaism at a time when the temple was still the great religious focus. They were joined by others with a variety of religious and cultural backgrounds, and Paul himself was continually adapting his own teaching as he met new situations. There were many preachers and many customs, and our canonical gospels come not only from a time when the Christian movement had to rethink its belief in the aftermath of the destruction of the temple but they present us with a variety of theologies. All the extant documents together from the first century and a half (whether they made it into the collection we call the New Testament or not) do not witness to all the diversity of practice and doctrine that existed.[5] It is little wonder that there have been so many competing visions all claiming "Paul," "the gospels," or "the tradition" as their justification. Unity is a desire, and we will only have it in its fullness at the heavenly banquet, toward which we must strive. Being in communion, living and working with every sister and brother, must be as much part of the moral agenda of each Christian as honesty and working for justice. We have a vision in the Christ, and we must work to realize it in his body that we are.

Unity as Omega, and Action Now

If we envision the unity of the body as part of the Omega toward which we journey, what does that demand as activity from me at next Sunday's gathering? If I should have a stable moral intention, a habit, that I will seek and work toward the unity of the whole body of the Christ, the

5. For a good example of this diversity, because it touched their practices when celebrating the Eucharist, see O'Loughlin 2018.

oikoumene, then I should, in love, presume that every other brother or sister has the same intention. Put negatively, I should give everyone the benefit of the doubt. I do this already with those who are baptized Catholics and stand around me. I know that if I were to examine them as to their doctrine, much less their doctrine regarding the eucharist, I would get an astonishing range of answers, yet we seek to act together. I know that likewise many of those around me would be surprised if they asked me similar questions, yet they would not dream of excluding me. This diversity of understandings is, indeed, already acknowledged in the liturgy by the fact that we have a homily—there is always room for growth in Christian understanding.

Now I see someone in the eucharistic gathering who is also a follower of Christ but not a member of the Catholic Church and my first thought must not be that this is a stranger or an alien, an interloper, but a sister or a brother. This is a real human being, beloved of the Father, not an embodiment of some defective theology. And, as such, I must hope that person is also moving toward the Omega-point. Presuming that, I must offer to share all I have with that person. If that person does not see him or herself on that path toward the goal of unity for which John presents the Lord praying (John 17:22), then that person can choose not to eat and drink with me—that is the individual's choice. But I must behave with the Omega-point as my goal and guide to action. And, given that this person has chosen to stand among us in our eucharistic action, I should be saddened if she or he then refused to eat and drink, for that now is a statement that building the links, the bonds, the sinews of the body of the Lord is not a priority. Yet being the body of the Lord is what we are deep down, and it is this reality that must be constantly growing and developing.

The situation presented by Anke de Bernardinis to Pope Francis in 2015 is a case in point. She said she had been "living happily" with her husband "for many years, sharing joys and sorrows," and so she found it "quite painful to be divided in the faith and to be unable to take part together in the Lord's Supper."[6] She has expressed the desire to build bonds. The bonds of marriage are a paradigm for those of the church and all these bonds form part of the web that is the *musterion* that will only become complete

6. See ch. 1 above.

and fully visible at the Omega-point.[7] I must presume here someone working toward that final goal of the Christ being all and in all (Col 3:11), and as such I must welcome her to the table fully as befits a sister. Not to do so would assume that I and my group, unlike her, had already reached the Omega-point—and that plainly is not the case for we still need to celebrate the liturgy of those still on the way to the eschaton.

What happens when I find myself among another group of Christians—for example, in a Methodist church—where I know that there would be little interest in many of the ideas about the papacy that Catholics hold dear and where there would not be an elaborate theology of presbyteral ministry in terms of sacerdotal powers? Rather than try to answer this abstractly I shall work my way through an actual situation that occurred for me about twenty years ago. My friends' baby boy was going to be baptized, and I was invited and was delighted to attend: rejoicing at a baptism is a basic Christian instinct and joining in the party at a baptism is a significant way of expressing our common joy at receiving adoption as children of God.[8] While I might skip a friend's housewarming if I had to go somewhere to give a lecture, I have always placed baptism alongside weddings and funerals as times "to be there"—and as a Christian theologian I see putting a baptism on a par with a wedding as a little aspect of my own witness. When I heard that the minister was going to have the baptism as part of the regular Sunday liturgy, I was further pleased as it showed that baptism was not being viewed as an individualist affair but as being welcomed into a church. On arrival, I discovered that that church's regular Sunday liturgy was a eucharist, and the presider explained at the beginning that while some visitors might not link together baptism and the eucharist, the connections were intimate. This, celebrating the eucharist, was the appropriate way for Christians to thank God for the gifts of children and of faith. Then she pointed out that baptism is the first step in initiation and the eucharist is the fullness of entering the church, that baptism is not a private family matter but an event of the church, and that the church is never more the church than when it celebrates the eucharist. She gave that community a fulsome rendering of our common Christian theology in a few user-friendly sentences. About that time there was a rather arid dispute when a Catholic bishop

7. See Eph 5:32.

8. See Gal 4:5.

objected to a Catholic politician who had taken communion in an Anglican liturgy, and at almost the same time surprise in the media when a Catholic priest very publicly rebuked a non-Catholic politician who went to communion with his Catholic wife. So I thought I should work through my options as I sat there in that Methodist church. Could I have refused to attend the baptism? No, because Christians should rejoice with their fellow disciples on such an occasion. Should they have "warned" everyone that it would be a eucharist, lest someone might not want to take part? No, because, first, every church is free to celebrate a baptism as it wishes; second, it is good liturgical practice to have a baptism at the regular Sunday eucharist, and indeed this is a growing together toward the unity for which the Lord prayed; and third, such a warning could be seen as encouraging division: everyone should act in a way that promotes the deepest bonds within the church giving fellow Christians the benefit of the doubt that they too would act in that way. So, if I had been minded to, was I free to choose not to eat and drink at this liturgy? In terms of raw possibilities I was, of course, free: I could walk out, I could just sit there and not move. But this is the same sort of freedom that would declare that I could tell a friend in need that I would not help. Responsible human freedom involves knowing that I can both damage and build, and it continuously chooses that which helps, builds, and gives light. Love and vocation limit my choices in that I must choose that which builds up the body of the Lord and express those links right now. While no one took notice that I did eat and drink, my friends would have noticed if I had not done so—and that act would have been a failure to testify to the journey upon which we are embarked of building bit by bit now the one, holy, catholic church. Therefore, the demands of building unity meant that, there and then, I had to eat and drink! And this moral responsibility is distinct from the human obligation to act with good manners when I am a guest at a meal.

A Catholic bishop once told me that it was "easy to be an ecumenist when sitting in the theologian's study," but very difficult when you were out working with people. I rather annoyed him when I said I thought it was the exact opposite. Sitting in the study one deals with abstract situations and with Catholic doctrine as a body of ideas, and one can list the difficulties of each position and add nuance upon nuance. In a community setting it is a matter of doing what is right because here you, as a real person, meet others, and it is the actual journey of faith, real life, we are making as distinct from just thinking of the journey. In the parish I must actually build up links toward unity rather than simply imagine them. Consequently, in actual life, I am never free to confess in the creed that I believe in the church's unity and then act in such a manner that one more little bond that could be established is not established. I am never free to declare I believe in the Catholic Church and commit an action that casts doubt on a sister's or brother's good faith that they too want to build the church. If I recite the creed and act differently, then I act inauthentically; I contradict my words with my deeds.

An Irony of Fraternal Love

Thus far in this chapter we have reflected on the fact that no Christian is ever a stranger to another, but that despite lots of deep differences in the way we do things and understand discipleship we are siblings on a journey—and we will all only be fully one in the Christ at the end. But, if we are brothers and sisters, is there not a much simpler way of approaching practice based on the nature of fraternal love?

The churches from the very beginning thought of themselves as not simply gatherings of people but as people who, through Jesus, were given a new relationship to their Father in heaven and to one another as sisters and brothers. We see this radically new way of thinking of one another at the end of 1 Thessalonians when Paul concludes with "Greet all the brothers with a holy kiss" (5:26) and elsewhere when he greets Phoebe, the deaconess at Cenchreae, as "our sister" (Rom 16:1). This language has survived in the liturgy of most churches (e.g., *Orate fratres*, pray, sisters and brothers) and as a specialist terminology within religious orders, but we should never forget that we are expected to behave within the church as among those with whom we are intimately connected. Moreover, the community of Christians is not simply a club—people with a common interest and purpose—but a group with a new vision of how we should relate to one another.

For an early teacher named John, from whose pen we have several early letters, this relationship of brotherhood and sisterhood with one another is a sacramental event:

> Whoever says, "I am in the light," while hating a brother or sister, is still in the darkness. Whoever loves a brother or sister lives in the light, and in such

> a person there is no cause for stumbling. But whoever hates another believer is in the darkness, walks in the darkness, and does not know the way to go, because the darkness has brought on blindness. (1 John 2:9-11)

and

> Those who say, "I love God," and hate their brothers or sisters, are liars; for those who do not love a brother or sister whom they have seen, cannot love God whom they have not seen. The commandment we have from him is this: those who love God must love their brothers and sisters also. (1 John 4:20-21)

The bonds of being siblings in the Lord is not simply a fact, but through loving my sister and brother visible beside me in the church I express my love for God. The sister or brother is there as a reality and our mutual love builds the kingdom now, but they are also a sacramental reality and through the mutual love we encounter the presence of God.[9] Loving one's siblings is a way of being in connection with God, far more than a moral rule for a happy society on the basis of "do as you would be done to." Appreciating that behaving toward other disciples as if they are brothers and sisters becomes one of the challenges of accepting the gospel. From this perspective much of the preaching in the gospels has to be understood as calling the early Christian audience to become aware of this relationship with their fellow Christians. In short, I must want the best for my brother and sister, appreciating that this new way of loving is the beginning of the reign of God.

The early communities found this call for brotherly love just as difficult as we do—hence the constant repetition of the need to see others in this way—but they did have one advantage. To them the language was new and shocking and so they were conscious of it as an aspect of the demands of the Christian lifestyle in a way that we are not. But now let us turn our attention to the one place—outside of full-time religious communities—where we encounter this language: the liturgy. There Christians will confess to "you my brothers and sisters," they will be asked to pray as sisters

9. This is, of course, a fundamental basis of the divine presence within the eucharistic assembly, but it would be a distraction from my argument to pursue this point here.

and brothers of the presider, they will pray at funerals for a brother or sister who has died, and there will be references here and there in homilies to our all being siblings in the Lord. For most people, most of the time, these references go by wholly unnoticed and are little more than the jargon of religion. But if liturgy is a serious business, as Catholics claim, then why do we refer to one another in this way? The most obvious answer is that this is a hangover from the early churches and is now little more than an anachronism that serves as a cultural distinguishing mark. The liturgy is full of these, as witness the vestments worn by presiders which are little more than a formalized vestige of higher-status Roman gentlemen in late antiquity,[10] and such language is simply there: it *means* nothing. As an explanation of the presence of this language this approach is solid, but there is much more going on in our liturgy than simply being a repository for nostalgic items from our past.

The liturgy sets up an alternative vision of living to that which we see around us in the everyday world.[11] It should model the lifestyle to which we as disciples aspire to live, and it should provide us with a physical glimpse of the world toward which we are on pilgrimage. We live in one world, but we discover other worlds in our imagination. Humans experience a world of meaningless strife, but in the story of Cain and Abel (Gen 4) we imagine another and remind ourselves that fratricide is the antithesis of God's plan. We live forgetting our neighbor, but in a story like that of the good Samaritan (Luke 10) we envisage another way of interacting with one another. We seek to be disciples and in the fraternal language of the liturgy we behave for a little while in a different way and

10. It was at this time that the eucharistic meal ceased being an evening event, a dinner, and became a breakfast given for clients. See Leonhard 2014.

11. Many object to seeing and treating others as brothers and sisters as specifically Christian, pointing out that *fraternité* was an Enlightenment value and that students join mutual support groups in colleges called fraternities and sororities. First, however, we should note that the sole ancient roots for this value of fraternity lie in the *fraternité* that was manifested in the liturgy and the monastic life; second, college groups are by their nature exclusive, whereas the problem for individual Christians in antiquity was that these links cut through the stratified society and were radically open: a slave whom you had never met could address you with a term of intimate equality as "brother"; and, last, Christians do not see these relationships as simply a functional interpersonal ethic but reflect an ontological reality in the process of coming to be, recognized now in faith.

imagine the world as we believe it should be. Just as love for a brother is sacramental of loving God, so the liturgy's use of this language is sacramental of Christian hope. But if this is the case, does it not pose a problem for anyone who would refuse to allow a sister or brother to share in the meal? If I call you a sister, I am obligating myself to behave in certain ways? Then, since I will act as a brother in every other way, I must be willing to act in a specific way at the eucharist and so share fully with you *all* that is on the table.

Moreover, if the liturgy is to remind us what should be and what will be—as in the way we call each other brothers and sisters—then must I not now make you fully my brother and sister by sharing my food and drink with you? Similarly, if I am present at another liturgy, one not organized by Catholics and presided over by someone who is a Catholic, must I not still act as a brother and sister and help us all to glimpse the world of fraternal unity for which the Lord prays?

We are faced with a choice. One option is to see the liturgy as a provisioning system organized by the group for the support of the individuals that make up the group. As such, the church is a cooperative. These are excellent organizations, and Christians should support any system that makes life easier for our fellow humans. But if the church is not more than this, we should abandon the trappings of family language as no more than an illusion that just adds to the level of deceit and deception in the world. We should get rid of all the family language such as "brother" and "sister" and referring to "our Father" in heaven. In such an organization we could have clear rules about belonging, here and now, post them on the notice board outside the building in which we assemble, and all will be well.

The other option is to see all this family language as part of the revelation to which we bear witness, which we grasp now in part but look forward to in its fullness. This partial, almost momentary, grasping of the world the Father intends is what we are engaged in when we assemble. The liturgy exists in the overlap between our everyday world and the world of the kingdom and within it a different logic of anticipatory imagination applies. Here each person is a sister or a brother and we gather with Jesus our brother who is also Lord and we address our Father as his adopted children. Here no one can be excluded as less a brother or sister without shattering the very nature of our assembly. Here no one can act in a way that disrupts the image of the family without undermining the very reason we are assembled as a liturgical community.

This argument is an argument from irony—if you are doing this, then you cannot behave is any other way that this—and it has a far better theological pedigree than many contemporary theologians recognize. My favorite example of the approach was that used by Luke in reference to prayer, and it is very apposite here.

> "What father among you, if his son asks for a fish, will instead of a fish give him a serpent; or if he asks for an egg, will give him a scorpion? If you then, who are evil, know how to give good gifts to your children, how much more will the heavenly Father give the Holy Spirit to those who ask him!" (Luke 11:11-13).

If fellow Christians asked us to share with them our earthly skills or possessions, we would not hesitate to see this as a moral imperative. So if we are sharing our sacramental riches as part of our common activity of bringing about the Father's kingdom, for whose coming we pray daily, then could we be justified in refusing full participation to a Christian sister or brother? And if I have prayed with others to *our* Father in heaven, and acknowledged myself as a brother when so addressed by you, can I refuse to share at the Christian family table without contradicting in action the very basis for my being there?

Respice Finem: Look toward the End

We should recall where we began this chapter with the world described by Paul in 1 Corinthians 11. We profess that we are "one in the Anointed One," but we also know that we are fractured people with fractious tendencies living in a fractured world where fractiousness and division hold only too much sway. However, we do not see this situation as either part of the nature of the universe (as, for example, Social Darwinians do) nor an inevitability consequent of a "fall" (as indeed do some Christians who imagine the universe through Hobbes's image that life is "brutish, nasty, and short" and for whom salvation is a wholly other worldly event unconnected with our activity now). So we must acknowledge problems and then move toward a better existence that will more adequately reflect the Father's will.

From within this cosmic vocation we can derive two liturgical principles affecting what we do next Sunday:

First, since any failure to build a bond between Christians or express in action our movement toward the Omega-point of the *oikoumene* negates our theological claim to believe that the unity of the church is the Lord's will for his people, we must presume that there is enough togetherness now such that every Christian present is welcome at our table. Likewise, I should not cause a disruption in the body of the Lord—if I am present at your eucharist and so, unless you, the hosts, say I am unwelcome, I should eat and drink.

Second, since our language of being brothers and sisters is a serious matter, part of our anticipation of the kingdom and part of our proclamation of the vision of the Lord for human life, I must recognize that I cannot treat you as a sister or brother without being willing to share my table with you. Likewise, I as your sibling must be willing to share your table.

4

Fictive Families—Real Churches

The Spirit and Intercommunion

In this time between Pentecost and the parousia, the Spirit is God's gift to the Church (cf. Rom. 5:5), bringing believers into relationship with God and one another and making it possible for them to love the Father through the Son.
—Anne McGowan[1]

In the last chapter we imagined the eucharist as a gathering of sisters and brothers around a table and then dwelt on this irony of calling someone beside you "sister" but then not being willing to eat alongside that person. But is that argument anything more than just the exploitation of a metaphor or an oddity of language? Has it any deep basis in our faith as Christians? It is to this question we now turn, and I shall argue that we are sisters and brothers united in the Christ, because the Holy Spirit is present and working within us when we gather for liturgy.

Telling a New Story

Whenever we meet an impasse in our relationships, our politics, or within our theology we are faced with an option. On the one hand we can attempt repetition upon repetition—and accept the consequences of the

1. McGowan 2014, 5.

resulting conflict. The alternative is to see if we can tell a new story of who we are and where we have come from such that the impasse is avoided. It is an assumption in this book that we are taking the latter path.

So where should we start in telling a new story about the eucharist? Since the eucharist is a ritual, we can begin by noting that "giving thanks" is a verb and that the eucharist is an action: it is the act of offering thanks to God. Moreover, this action of thanking God takes the form not just of words but of another basic human action: having a meal. Here is a starting point that is not only attested in our stories but one that is found in our humanity. We have already looked at this in chapter 2, but let us reframe the story here.

These two related activities, thanking God and sharing meals, are neither arbitrary nor insignificant activities, but at the core of the human being as a creature. A creature is never more true to the creaturely state of being than in thanking the Source of All for that by which existence is held in the living state: food. Likewise, thanking God for food is an activity that we find not only in our own history—it is placed at the beginning of our mythic history in Gen 4:2-5—but is found across the religious spectrum. One has but to look at the various manifestations of petitions for the harvest and then the festival at its completion. This action of being thankful for food may have so changed over time that many who are most familiar with the recent ritual are uneasy at the sight of the basic action.[2] But rather than seeing origins as merely a primitive *locus* for an ideal today, we can see in the origins of the ritual a recall to basic purposes. It may be that the action that called the ritual into being is now completely otiose—and its continuance is because it serves some new purpose; or that the action is still as necessary as ever; or that it is so encrusted with later layers as to be invisible; or, indeed, that all is just as it should be. However, searching for the basic rationale of the action is a valuable activity for all engaged in the ritual. And we still need food and, as believers in a Creator, still need to be thankful.

2. There is a widely held view that the meal setting of the eucharist was but a convenient occasion for something quite distinct from the meal, or that the meal was merely a temporary wrapper for a more spiritual reality—see, for example, Ratzinger 2000, 7–8—but this view not only fails to do justice to the historicity of the incarnation, but it sets a low value on the whole significance of meals in the preaching and memory of Jesus. On this see D. E. Smith 2003.

Second, we need to seek out stories that not only are true to the fundamental action but can fit with our larger narratives of who we are as the people of God. Our stories on particular matters are only as good as their ability to form an integrated story with the gospel, albeit one that is always incomplete. Moreover, in the case of stories that seek new beginnings after divisions, the stories told must be equally applicable to both sides of the division. This is where most ecumenical dialogue on intercommunion falls totally flat. The Catholic side seeks desperately to find some way by which they could admit an outsider to their eucharist—and imagine that all is well when that occurs. But the issue of whether or not the Catholics can participate in another church's eucharist hardly occurs—and when it is brought up, they revert to a position that is tantamount to saying "the others have no eucharist!" as discussed in chapter 1.

A Starting Point in Anthropology

Can we sketch out a new story, even in brief? One obvious starting point is with the place of food in human life: not only is it the *sine qua non* [most literally], but is it at the heart of all human culture—a matter we looked at, in a different way, in chapter 2. It was Plutarch (second century CE) who pointed out that "we invite each other to meals not for the sake of eating and drinking, but for eating and drinking together."[3] Sharing food not only fosters sociability, it creates society. We are not simply what we eat, nor are we simply animals that form combinations for feeding purposes: *we are beings who share meals.* Meal-sharing is as defining a characteristic of humanity as one can find.[4]

3. Plutarch, *Quaestiones conviviales* 2.10 (643).

4. The classic Boethian definition, *individua substantia rationalis naturae*, used to take its empirical starting point from the simplest evidence for inferential thinking: tool-making—if one found tools, then one had the genus *homo*. This, a commonplace in books on human origins of a generation ago, has been found to be inadequate with advances in primatology that show such basic tool-using rationality among the apes. But, to my knowledge, while food procurement is a shared, and learned, activity among the apes, we have no evidence that food-sharing is a cultural phenomenon in the way it is among humans. However, the basic conclusion seems secure: food-sharing is a more characteristic defining difference for the identification of the human than rationality.

On this relationship of humanity and sharing food it is easy to miss two salient facts. First, by far the largest portion of all human effort down the centuries has been devoted to obtaining, processing (virtually everything other than certain fruits needs processing), and consuming food. Second, we are the only animals who cook our food. Therefore, food is necessarily social, a part not just of human activity but of culture, a part of our memory and identity.[5] We share food not just with our blood relatives, the biological family, but in establishing humans bonds: the sharing becoming both the means and the reality of larger gatherings. These gatherings are not simply agglomerations but, however fleeting, communities.

We can think of the very stable communities built around eating such as the sergeants' mess, the annual dinner-dance of the golf club, or the refectory of a religious institute. But we can also think about the fleeting communities of the families and friends of the couple at a wedding reception (one of the basic human rites of passage that is cemented by a meal of distinct families),[6] the shared food at a conference, or simply in terms of those who "do lunch" as part of their networking. Around the shared food a community, a fictive family, is called into existence. We belong to any number of these fictive families, for sharing food transforms us from being isolated individuals to being part of this and then of that community, while we are also aware of those more stable communities where we belong—and in those communities we will usually have memories of shared meals. Can you imagine any significant celebration without a feast? We could use a shorthand from Christian tradition and see the sharing of food as the natural sacrament of human community. Now bear in mind that one of the ways that the followers of Jesus thought about themselves was as guests at a feast.[7]

But shared meals are not only at the base of society, they are found across the religious spectrum of humankind. Indeed, as soon as one looks at a religion as anything more than a set of abstract ideas one is led quickly from the library into the kitchen. There are special foods for this feast or that group, foods to be avoided always or for a specific time, festivals that need food for special banquets, and there is a detailed appreciation of the links between certain foods and certain meals. We might think of the lamb that was prescribed for the Passover meal (Exod 12), while, being of a somewhat traditional bent myself, I cannot imagine a Christmas

5. See O'Loughlin 2015, 61–94.

6. See Charsley 1992.

7. See Wolter 2009.

lunch without a plum pudding and brandy butter! Moreover, there are not just all the things that happen with food, shared food is an ubiquitous theme in religious stories: we need only recall the story of Abraham's feast for the strangers (Gen 18) or Jesus' parables involving feasts. Religious memory, sharing food, and cultural and community memory are not merely overlapping categories but overlapping realities.

For our purposes, ancient Judaism supplies both a relevant—for it constituted the meal awareness of Jesus and his followers—and convenient—for we all have access to the basic texts in our Bibles—source of examples. Moreover, the connections between religion and food can be observed at many levels both in practice and story. In practice there are the festival meals—explicitly linked to the liturgical year just as it was, in many cases, originally linked to the annual cycle of food production. We can think of it also in terms of the temple rituals; the sacrifices were imagined as presenting and sharing a meal with the Lord: many offerings were shared between the offerer, the priests, and the Lord whose altar (physically a giant elevated bonfire) was imagined as his table. God not only accepted his share of food, but even of beer![8] Every sacrifice of thanksgiving involved not just that which was the Lord's portion, but involved a meal of the community.[9] The banquet—so familiar to us because of its place in early Christian story—was a central element in Jewish story: the Lord would gather his scattered people and provide for them the banquet of banquets.[10] But the links between food and religion were most often seen at the domestic level: the great occasional meals assumed the regularity of the Sabbath-eve meal, and that meal assumed that every meal was graced by thanksgiving. One was not to eat without blessing the Lord.[11] To belong to the community of the covenant was to thank God for his goodness in providing food. And so we find guidance, in the book of Sirach, for a young man on how to bless God for food at a banquet so that he does it properly, but without droning on;[12] we have the descriptions of the first sung eucharistic prayers in the descriptions of the meals

8. See Homan 2004.

9. Josephus, *The Antiquities of the Jews* 3, 224–26; and see O'Loughlin 2015, 131–34.

10. For example, Isa 25:6; 55:1-2; see Marshall 2009.

11. Bokser 1981; O'Loughlin 2012.

12. Sir 31:12–32:13—and note that there are echoes of this in early Christian writings (e.g., 1 Cor 10:7; Luke 10:8); see Smit 2011, who describes this Sirach passage as the "cultural encyclopedia" of the early followers of Jesus in their meal practices.

of the Therapeutae;[13] while the first texts[14] of Christian eucharistic prayers we possess come from the *Didache* where some texts are provided, for committal to memory and use by those who, taking a lead at a community meal / Eucharist, do not have the abilities of the prophets to improvise.[15] If meals are central to our humanity and society, then it is equally true they are central to our specific religious inheritance.

But surely there are more significant religious activities than "saying grace" for food which, for most of us, seems overly pious, is often slightly embarrassing, and when done is often formulaic and perfunctory? Surely 'Eucharist' must have another starting point? In contrast to the widely held perceptions we might note three points. First, a fundamental element of our faith is that we are creatures, dependent for our being, absolutely, upon God.[16] We are equally dependent for our actual existence on food. Though this sense of dependence is lost to a large extent within our society, that does not gainsay the reality. Therefore, making ourselves keenly aware of this at the heart of our worship is to be very well grounded in our divinely dependent ontology.[17] Second, the basic attitude of creatures is that of thanksgiving in the midst of the realization of dependence. To thank God is an acknowledgment not only of God's goodness and mercy but of our situation. As the third Eucharistic Prayer in *The Roman Missal* states: "you are worthy of praise from every creature which has its being from you."[18] Third, celebration is the fundamental note of our existence not only following from our acknowledgment that God is good and all that is created is good, very good (Gen 1), but our joy that we are a reborn and re-created people in the Christ.

From Meal to Church

But if every shared meal of a gathering is a fictive family and a human unity, is it simply a case that if they are Christians, then that meal is a

13. Philo, *De vita contemplativa* 64–78; see O'Loughlin 2015, 84–87.

14. We do not have any recorded words of blessing in the gospels, but only the words addressed to the audience about what to do; see O'Loughlin 2014.

15. *Didache* 10.7.

16. This is the significance of the shorthand *creatio ex nihilo*.

17. Indeed, the preaching of this dependence may be part of our ecological responsibility: this is our *Sitz-im-Leben* affecting our *kerugma*.

18. *et merito te laudat omnis a te condita creatura.*

church? (Church being, in this case, simply a religious "take" on a human reality.) First, let us acknowledge that this is a real human unity when a group shares food, but to be a church is something *more*: it is an identity both before others and before God. This transformation from fictive family to the people of God is the work of the Spirit. It is the Spirit's hovering that transforms us from being a unified people to being a people united in Christ in praise of the Father. A church—an actual gathering of disciples—is never simply a product of human effort but the work of the Spirit. Curiously, we forget this when we think of a church as an assembly of the baptized (or those baptized into a particular communion) or when we use phrases like "no priest, no eucharist; no eucharist, no church." But an assembly, however unified, becomes the people of the covenant through the Spirit. It is the Spirit who enables us to see through the dark glass of the world of signs to the realities of the divine; it is the Spirit who inspires our memories so that our recollection is not simply a reverie but a participation in the reality remembered: "by the Spirit's power, you Lord give all life and holiness and gather a people to yourself."[19]

We have created many theologies of the eucharist that have either marginalized the Spirit—the Roman Canon never mentioned the Spirit and can only be said to have an epiclesis by a very accommodating reading—or packaged the role of the Spirit to a specific role in the action that, for Catholics, was not to be seen to cut across the operative force of the words of consecration uttered by a validly ordained priest. But any new story of the eucharist, which takes its basis in its origins as a meal of the disciples, must equally present it as the meal of the church through the presence of the Spirit in the individuals and in the community.

Over the past millennium Western eucharistic theology has been fascinated with change, transformation, and movement. How does one change bread and wine? Does it really change? How does it change? Who has the power to change it? Is the change a form of motion? Is the change, if there is a change, an action of a power or simply a request? If it is a power, how does it reside in the power holder? If it is a change, is it a substantial change? If it is a substantial change, what happens to the substances? Is it an instantaneous change? When does the change occur? The list of questions goes on and on until it reaches some of the more silly questions that have divided Christians in the past and which continue

19. Eucharistic Prayer 3: *Domine . . . Spiritus Sancti operante virtute, vivificas et sanctificas universa, et populum tibi congregare non desinis.*

to divide them. When I am speaking to a group and some such question arises, my heart sinks because once this approach is taken, there is always another question lurking in the background demanding ever-greater precision. The reason the questioning never reaches a fully satisfactory conclusion—and so a position all Christians could agree upon or even a position that all the members of a single denomination could agree upon—is that it assumes that our liturgical activity is akin to physics rather than to music, poetry, or painting. Liturgy, and preeminently the eucharist, is part of the poetry that uses the words, actions, and realities of this world of sight, touch, and taste to encounter the world beyond, the mystery of God's love for us, and *the* mystery: God. This is the nature of saying that the liturgy is sacramental. A meal that makes me fictively a brother or sister with other creatures whom I can feel at my elbow in a church building can also make me really a brother or sister of each of them as children of the Father in his kingdom.

So consider these changes. Anyone can see that a gathering in a building is a collective affair: an obvious indication is that they sing together. So they can really and honestly say that "we are singing"—there is an "us" in a far more profound way than we can say of all the people in a large shop. Everyone in the shop has a shared purpose for being there: to shop. But they form an "us" in a very accidental way in that we do not know whether they share values, ideas, or desire for the company of the other people there: they just all happen to be there at the same time. Now the group who is singing has come precisely because that is when the group assembles—they share beliefs, they share beliefs about who they are, and they are engaged in a single common task. But what transforms that human group into being something beyond sight and sound: the body of the Christ? *This* change takes the group from being a reality of this world and makes it a reality within the divine plan. Invisibly, without any outward indication, the group can say both "We are a group singing as part of a religious ritual" and "We are Christ's body who are singing through, with, and in him to the Father." This transformation is the work of the Spirit.

It is the Spirit who changes the group from being a family only in a figurative, fictive sense into being the actual family that is the people of God. The words we use become prayers in the power of the Spirit, and we are changed as we stand and use those words from being a group engaged in reflection on the human condition to a priestly people placing those needs before the Father through the Spirit. It is the Spirit who forms us into a communion, and changed our location, in the deepest sense, from standing simply there to being located in the heavenly sanctuary. It is because of the Spirit's presence that it is our meal and it is the heavenly banquet. So whenever disciples gather to pray, it is the Spirit's presence that makes that gathering a real church, part of *the* church. "The Church, as the community of the new covenant, confidently invokes the Spirit, in order that it may be sanctified and renewed, led into all justice, truth and unity, and empowered to fulfil its mission in the world."[20] Any and all of these transformations, these sacramental changes, are but aspects of the Spirit's presence. But if it is the Spirit of God that is bringing about all these changes, then the Spirit's work demands we change how we view the issue of intercommunion.

And of Intercommunion?

We have already seen that a meal is a ritual with its own grammar and expectations—this is a reality we must not only acknowledge but honor as part of the plan of creation. I cannot share a meal with you, or you with me, or either of us with a community if I refuse to eat or refuse your eating with me. Can one imagine being allowed to come to a party and then being told: "You may not eat!"? Can you imagine letting someone come to your table and then refusing to share with them? Such behavior breaks the grammar of meals and a most basic human code.[21] But this human reality becomes, in the Spirit's power, a sacramental reality and an encounter with God and his Christ. It is this working of the Spirit that is ignored by those who set up a gulf or an opposition between the eucharist as "meal" and the eucharist as "sacrament." The community meal is sacramental, the human bonding is real, and is sometimes felt as *communitas*, and the bonding in Lord Jesus is real, and in faith we perceive the body of the Lord. This must not be seen as just one kind of bonding that is then followed by another; rather it is all the work of the Spirit bringing us toward our finality. A human encounter is simultaneously a divine encounter for the Spirit, in that great image from Genesis, hovers over the whole of the creation.

So if the Spirit is joining us together, then not sharing with one of those in whom the Spirit is working is a rejection of the Spirit. I cannot claim

20. *BEM*, Eucharist II, C, 17—the whole section entitled "The Eucharist as Invocation of the Spirit' (Eucharist, II, C, 14–18) is worthy of study.

21. See ch. 2 above.

that the Spirit is present in our gathering making it a sacramental encounter and then not share with you because this would be declaring a boundary between us when the Spirit is establishing a bond. We are faced with a stark choice. One can *either* have signs up outside saying "Only such-and-such kinds of Christians, in good standing, can enter here" (and there have been many cases of this in the past), which is tantamount to saying that the Spirit's working is limited to those who share our visible ecclesial belonging, *or* one can offer welcome to all who come to the gathering—because the call to join with us is recognized in faith as ultimately from the Spirit. The welcome is a visible recognition by a church of the Spirit being at work in the heart of each one of the gathering. Unless the Spirit is moving within someone's heart one would not find this gathering worthwhile nor would one express any desire to eat with us. Therefore, intercommunion is an acknowledgement of the Spirit's presence and work within a deeply human ritual.

But what is the situation when I find myself at a meal of another church, another community, where I have been welcomed or at least not excluded? Again, if it is the Holy Spirit who is making this human gathering a gathering of Christians, in whose power this actual assembly is a church praising and thanking the Father in the Christ, then my participation in eating and drinking is my acknowledgement of the Spirit at work in the community and my own reaction to the Spirit at work within me. If I were not to join in this meal I would deny that I am really present as a fellow Christian; it would make me simply an observer of *their* activity not of what *we* are doing. This distinction is worth thinking about. Let us imagine I was sent to spy on a group of Christians to see what they were up to—we have the famous case from the early second century when Pliny the Younger as governor of Bithynia investigated a eucharistic gathering and found it to be to his eyes a "harmless" meal[22]—then I would not be really there and could not say in my heart "we are praying" but would be just pretending that I was a member of that community. Now if there is pretense involved, then it is the very opposite of cooperating with the Spirit who is the Spirit of truth (John 14:17), the One who brings us into contact with deep reality

22. Pliny the Younger, *Epistulae* 10.96 (8): *Quibus peractis, morem sibi discedendi fuisse rursusque coeundi ad capiendum cibum promiscuum tamen et innoxium*. The governor does not dignify this gathering as a meal (*cena*) such as his class ate: it is simply a gathering for taking food—and, so, more like the common feeding of slaves or beasts.

(John 16:13), and the one who intercedes when we try to pray with sighs too deep for words (Rom 8:26). If I am pretending it is a "we," then I should depart at once and seek forgiveness for my false witness. But imagine that an anthropologist came to that assembly as part of a study of the structure of that liturgical assembly and, as the jargon has it, was located "on the balcony," looking in on the assembly *rather than* being a participant. This is a perfectly acceptable position to take, but it should be labeled as such: I should say "I am here but only as an observer," and I am not praying with you and so I am not acknowledging the divine in this situation. But if I am there and do take part recognizing this as an encounter of a community with God—for example, if I were to join in the Lord's Prayer—then I must acknowledge that the Spirit is at work here. This is not simply a human meal; it is a church's eucharist, and I as a Christian am a part of this church right now—because the Spirit is making us, myself and those around me, into the body of the Christ.

This chapter is not intended as a finished argument; its aim is to suggest that a starting point within the anthropology of meals has much to recommend it in that it looks to our origins and the example of Jesus and is located within created nature; and that if we seek a new story to fulfill a basic longing of the eucharist, that we might be one with the Lord at his table, then that story may lead us to thinking about the Spirit in our life in a new way that might repair a gap in our thinking of the eucharist—and then might show us another way to think about intercommunion. This new story that starts with anthropology and ends with pneumatology, starts with a human meal and ends with a sacramental meal, follows the sure dynamic of creation that "grace builds upon nature." That such a new story is needed was implicitly recognized in the encounter between Anke de Bernardinis and Pope Francis in November 2015, just as it was recognized in this prayer from a time when the eucharist was a real banquet with many stories of its significance:

> Remember, O Lord God, your church
> Deliver her from evil
> Complete her in your love
> and gather her from the four winds into your kingdom
> which you have prepared for her
> for yours is the power and the glory forever (*Didache* 10:5).

5

The Ecumenical Meal of Mission

But you, O God, are uniquely the most generous giver of all that is good.
—Augustine[1]

In the previous chapters we have looked at what happens to us as human beings around a table, how we become sisters and brothers through the transformative work of the Spirit, and we have suggested that the eucharistic banquet is part of the divine mission that leads us from the simplest gathering to the heavenly banquet. But that begs two questions. First, is there any basis in our tradition for seeing the Christian meal as part of the mission of God and the church. Put another way, while we have seen the eucharist as the outcome of mission, the achievement of discipleship, in that we have fenced it off for those in a state of grace and in peace and communion with the Apostolic See, can we look to any background of the eucharistic meal being used to embrace those who are not yet fully in communion with us and by embracing them in our welcome fostering the Lord's mission "that they might be one" (John 17:11)? And, second, if the relationship of being sisters and brothers in the Lord Jesus is fostered in our eating and drinking together, then is this simply a result of our common beliefs and actions—as it certainly is—or is it even more deeply

1. Augustine, *Confessiones* 2.6.13.

embedded within the saving work of Jesus, which constitutes us as New People? In short, how is who we are at the table a consequence of who we are as the baptized? These two questions are interconnected because they are aspects of a larger issue: What constitutes the real boundaries of the people who assemble to celebrate the eucharist? We usually locate any discussion touching on baptism at the outset of our discourse, but here I will begin with mission in this chapter—because kerugma preceded entering the mystery—and then look at baptism in the next chapter.

So, can we look to our memory for a story of how sharing food could break existing boundaries and establish in that table fellowship a new boundary of the people of God? If we look at Acts 10–11:18 we can see Luke presenting us with a series of meals he considers of importance in his vision of a world church: one that reaches from Jerusalem out to the ends of the earth. Moreover, these meals were recalled by him in such a manner that they were intended to challenge the already received wisdom of the churches in which his stories were being heard. Recalling the structure and salient points of Luke's narrative allows us to speculate on some of the tensions present in early communities, while offering us material for reflection on our own ecumenical practice.

Peter's Meals: Clean Food, Clean People

Acts 10:1–11:18 is conventionally seen as forming a unit within a larger set of stories about Peter as a missionary (9:31–11:18), and this particular section is usually characterized not in terms of meals but in terms of its final outcome: the conversion of Cornelius and his household.[2] However, instead of reading the story as one about conversion or indeed its immediate context in the churches where Luke was being read, where it was probably related to the disputes between Jewish-Christians and Gentile-Christians about keeping the purity laws, one can read it as a story about how food was used in the churches. The basis for this shift in emphasis is provided in the text itself, when at 10:28 Peter is presented as declaring that no person is "common" (*koinos* in the sense of "profane") or unclean on the basis of his previous vision that no food is common or unclean (10:14). Luke is, therefore, thinking simultaneously about food and people. So, reversing

2. See, for example, Dillon 1990, 725.

the interpretation of the images, we can read the whole story in terms of food, its consumption, and how the table manners of those who follow Jesus can be, in this story, a guide to Christian action.

The scene is set in 10:1-9 when a Roman soldier—who is neither a Jew nor a Gentile follower of Jesus—is praying at the ninth hour and is told by an angel that because of his righteous human behavior (10:4) his path and that of Simon Peter would cross. This means that he will be brought within the new covenant community (Luke 22:20) through an apostle: Peter (Acts 1:2). The backstory complete, Luke now tells the main story beginning with a hungry Peter.

Peter is at the sixth hour praying and becomes hungry, so he wants something cooked for him, and for this he has to wait. Luke just takes it for granted that we understand that when an apostle wants food there is some sort of provisioning service available to him—and we must recall that Peter is not in his own home but a guest lodging with Simon the tanner in Joppa (Acts 10:6). However, the guidance offered on how followers of The Way are to receive visiting "apostles and prophets" in the *Didache* illumines the situation. Normally, these guests are not to stay more than one or two days (Acts 9:43 tells us Peter had stayed there some time, no doubt due to his special position as a leader among the apostles), but any apostle or prophet is to be welcomed "as if they were the Lord." Clearly, these guests often asked their hosts to provide them with food, because the *Didache* reminds communities that they are to be given just enough food when they leave to sustain them until their next lodging, and communities are to be suspicious of those who order a banquet for themselves "in the spirit."[3] It was, therefore, taken for granted that Peter, an apostle, would be provided with the food he needed while a guest, and indeed that he had simply to ask for it from his hosts' hospitality! It is also clear that other apostles—a much larger group than the Twelve—were abusing the customs that we see taken for granted here in Acts—and hence the *Didache* has to offer warning advice to communities. One other point needs to be noted: this household in which Peter is lodging is a Jewish household (as we should expect given that this tanner is named Simon), and the food that would be provided would be lawful in accordance with purity and food customs that claimed their basic authority from Lev 11:2-23 and

3. See *Didache* 11:1-9.

Deut 14:3-20. Everything is, in other words, proceeding according to the Torah and the expected customs: "situation normal."

While Peter awaits his hosts' provision of food, something happens. Luke wants us to imagine this as explicitly out of the ordinary for he tells us that Peter fell into "an ecstasy" and so this does not belong to the world of rational discourse or the cultural world of Joppa. A great square sheet full of impure animals is lowered down before him, and all these animals are offered to Peter as a divine gift of food. The four-cornered sheet is meant to bring to our minds a tablecloth and all that is akin to a banquet of many meats suitable for a feast,[4] and it can be taken as implying the whole living world as created.[5] Peter is to kill and eat but refuses for he rejects—and always has until this moment in his life—that which is common (*koinos*) and unclean. Now the voice tells him that God makes all clean, so to call any food "common" is to be untrue to reality—even if (we are to infer) such a statement would be true to the law. Just so that we know this is a serious message we are then told it happened three times—in the narrative world of the early Christians important moments need to be produced in triplicate.[6] But despite the repetition, the significance of the vision of all this food offered from heaven for his hunger was not immediately apparent to Peter for, fully awake and back in the world of Joppa, he was "greatly perplexed" (10:17).

At this point the three people sent by Cornelius appear outside and Peter is told by the Spirit that he is to go with them without hesitation—but before they went anywhere, Peter (a lodger himself in Simon's house) "invited them in and he received them as guests" (10:23). Peter the guest has now turned into the host, and he extends a welcome to others. This shift in status to make Peter the primary agent of what is happening is

4. See Wolter 2009. We must avoid thinking that there was some formal distinction (a retrojection of later liturgical experience in the churches) between feasts, community meals, and specifically religious gatherings for the eucharist: the core eucharistic activity—blessing the Father for his goodness in the Christ—was part of the communities' regular gatherings to eat, and this feast was seen in continuity with all the meals of Jesus.

5. The language of Acts 10:12 echoes Gen 1:24-30; Luke also appears to be using a rhetorical commonplace in mentioning (a) four-footed animals, (b) reptiles, and (c) birds. Paul gives a similar list in Rom 1:23.

6. See Luke 20:12; 22:34, 61; Mark 14:41; Matt 26:44; and John 21:17.

demanded by the nature of Luke's message: Peter is taking a decisive step and he is fully responsible for it. But what is this step—surely "giving them lodging" (a common translation) is no more than practical hospitality or, in our parlance, "putting them up for the night"—in view of the fact that they have a long journey to Caesarea to make the next day? But this is far more than just finding them a bed. What is implicit in welcoming them as guests—sharing not only the house space but the table in the house—is spelled out a little later: Peter will be criticized for having dealings with the uncircumcised and for eating with them (11:3), and he will say that at the very moment he met these messengers that "the Spirit told [him] to go with them and not to make a distinction between them and us" (11:12). In effect, in welcoming these messengers as guests Peter has recognized that one can eat—precisely because the Spirit has revealed it—with any of God's creatures because this too has been revealed: no one is common or unclean (10:28). It is with these three anonymous messengers—two slaves and a pious soldier—that Luke imagines The Way moving beyond the confines of the people of Israel and the boundaries of the Torah. And that boundary is transgressed in an act of welcoming and table-sharing. Thus Peter—and so all apostles—are expected to continue the boundary-breaking commensality that was an important theme in Luke's portrayal of Jesus: "This fellow welcomes sinners and eats with them" (Luke 15:2).[7]

Two days later Peter and Cornelius meet in Caesarea, and they begin to talk. Lest the significance of what had already happened in Joppa (when Peter entertained the Gentile messengers) and of what was now happening in Caesarea be lost on his audience, Luke spells out the settled position of the Jerusalem church explicitly. Peter speaks to the assembled Gentile household—a group that already looks like "a church"[8] because they are said to be "in the presence of God" (Acts 10:33)]: "You yourselves know that it is unlawful for a Jew to associate with or to visit a Gentile; but God has shown me that I should not call anyone profane or unclean" (10:28). Peter is now formally acknowledging what those who were attentive in the audience have already realized: since he welcomed those messengers

7. One can find the theme of Jesus' open commensality throughout Luke's gospel. See D. E. Smith 1987 and 1989; O'Loughlin 2013.

8. See Trebilco 2011.

as guests, Peter has been living in a new cosmos where nothing can be called common because all is made good by God.

Cornelius then tells his part of the story (10:30-33), and Peter replies with a "history of salvation" sermon (10:34-43) such as Luke places in his mouth on several occasions in Acts.[9] But there are two variants. First, previous speeches have been addressed to the people of Israel, this is addressed to the righteous in every nation—because he now recognizes that God does not have favorites (10:35). Second, for the first time the appearance of the risen Jesus contains a reference to the theme of the postresurrection meals:[10] the witnesses to the resurrection are those who ate and drank with Jesus then (10:41). Encountering the risen Lord is a meal-sharing experience, which would have been heard by Luke's audience in terms of their own eucharistic meal-sharing.[11] Moreover, eating is not simply a matter of nourishment or a matter of law keeping: eating and drinking together identifies people (in this case as specially chosen witnesses [10:41]), and it is a means of establishing the eschatological community. Sharing food and drink is a serious religious engagement: it can join Jew with Jew, Jew with Gentile, and the disciple with the Lord.

When Peter had finished his speech, the Holy Spirit fell on the group—much to the surprise of the six Jewish Christians (11:12) that had traveled with Peter—and so it was evident that "the Holy Spirit had been poured out even on the Gentiles" (10:44-45). Then the household was baptized, and Peter and the other Jewish Christians lived as guests in that Gentile household (10:48). But such radical action demands a reckoning and so the story now moves back to Jerusalem (11:1), where Peter gives an account of what has happened by retelling the vision of the sheet full of animals offered him as food (11:5-10). This retelling repeats the message that all is created clean and so should not be called common (11:9), and so there is no basis for the objection made against him that he should not have eaten with the uncircumcised (11:3). Eating together is seen as responding to the divine initiative and to establish a bond that is more profound than circumcision: indeed, eating ordinary food—for no food

9. Acts 2:14-40 is the most exemplary of these "history of salvation" speeches.

10. See O'Loughlin 2009.

11. Luke's Emmaus story (Luke 24) is his paradigm for the presence of the risen Lord in the churches' meal-sharing.

is common or unclean—together forms the actual bond of the ecumenical community of the risen Christ.

Trances, Voices, and Angels

One of the most significant features of the whole story is the density of divine interventions—in one form or another—that characterize the story. It might be objected that such miraculous elements are found throughout Acts—the ascension of Jesus into the clouds (1:9), the destruction of Ananias and Sapphira (5:5 and 5:10), the vision of Stephen (7:55), or Paul's handkerchiefs (19:12)—but not with such connected frequency. Indeed, the web of references to otherworldly events, and the repetition of these references, suggest that Luke wants us to be more aware here than elsewhere of the otherworldly nature of the task of the apostles and the churches.

The first event is the vision of an angel of God—as "a man in dazzling clothes" standing before him "in his house" given to the Gentile, Cornelius. This "holy angel" (10:22) then speaks to him with his message that God has seen his righteousness. We are told this in Luke's voice from his perfect knowledge as the all-seeing narrator (10:3-7); then it is repeated by the messengers, as a report of an event, for Peter's benefit by the messengers (10:22); then it is repeated again by Cornelius himself in an *oratio recta* that reaffirms it and shows that he has understood its full import (10:30-32); and finally we hear it a fourth time: when Peter in his own voice repeats Cornelius's account (11:13-14), and thus affirms to his narrative audience that this vision has divine credentials. This angelic visitation is thus one of the most attested events in the whole story of Acts.

The second event is the trance and vision of Peter where he hears a voice that comes from heaven (10:10-16). Having been given the story in Luke's voice as narrator, it is repeated for us, almost verbatim, as Peter's own experiences (11:5-10). From the audience's perspective this not only allows Luke to repeat the key message but within the logic of the narrative allows him to present Peter owning this vision and so all that is implied in it and all that Peter will infer from it. Moreover, we the audience have already been given an advantage in understanding in comparison with the disciples in Jerusalem in that Peter has already narrated this as an action of God in his speech to Cornelius's household when he said that "but God has shown me that I should not call anyone profane or unclean" (10:28).

The third event is when the Spirit speaks to Peter about the messengers and how he is to react to them. This is told to us first in Luke's voice (10:19), and then we hear Peter's recollection (11:12), which makes explicit what is implied in the Spirit's message when it is told to us by Luke. Through this rhetorical device we do not merely have to take the divine decision on Luke's authority, but we have Peter openly declaring that the Spirit told him that he was not to make a distinction between Jew and Gentile. And practically this meant that he was not to make such a distinction at table—which is the very action that has prompted an accusation against him (11:3) and this defense.

The fourth event is that "the Holy Spirit fell upon all who heard the word" (10:44). This is then acknowledged—and so repeated—as a fact by Peter (10:47), then recalled in Jerusalem (11:15); and repeated yet again as part of the overall conclusion of the story (11:17-18). We, the audience, can be under no doubt that this whole sequence of events begins with God and not with a human situation (contrast Mark 7:24-30), is made explicit in its significance by prophetic means, and that it is to be considered significant in memory through its multiple iterations in the narrative.

So why has Luke used so much repetition? This pattern of repetition allows his audience to hear the story at three levels. Most simply we have the account of the narrator, Luke, coming directly to us as a series of connected details set in a temporal sequence over a matter of days that we are simply expected to appreciate as historical facts. Within this narrator's level the repetitions are set merely as recollections, at specific points, of earlier events in the sequence. Then, second, we have the direct testimony of the characters in their own voices as they declare the otherworldly acts of which they are witnesses. This is their declaration of the works of God, and on the basis of their witness we, the audience, are expected to affirm the veracity of the details of the story. The third level is the act of repetition itself, which takes historical form in the recollection by Peter when he has returned to Jerusalem, and this is presented as being read into the record of the whole church. Thus the repetition, most significantly in Peter's "orderly account" (11:4) as we find it in 11:5-17, is the formal ecclesial memory of an event of revelation. Once this orderly account is received, it is accepted by the church as the will of God made manifest (11:18). Meanwhile, the audience hearing this are expected to realize that they too must acknowledge the story and hold it as part of their own memory as disciples.

Customary Background

Luke's story presupposes that the issue of how disciples eat with one another is one that he considers of importance. Apart from what he tells us in the story about hesitations among Jewish followers of The Way about eating with Gentiles we have some other hints that throw light on the story.[12] The *Didache* assumes that Gentiles can become part of The Way of Life, and also that with regard to food regulations people should do what they are able to do (6:3), and so, by implication, everything less than the Torah is to be seen as a concession. As such, it can be seen as an expression of Jewish Christianity,[13] such as we see in Peter at the time he went into the ecstasy (Acts 10:14), his somewhat startled companions (10:45), and, more explicitly, his Jerusalem accusers (11:3). That such a customary background as we find in the *Didache* is the setting for Luke's story is made more plausible not only because of the way Peter behaves in Simon the Tanner's house, as noted above, but also by the fact that Peter is praying at the sixth hour, while Cornelius is praying at the ninth hour—such a pattern is consistent with that prescribed in *Didache* 8:3. However, there is a hesitation in the *Didache* in that it assumes that only those who are already baptized can join in the meals of the community (9:5), and it would be anachronistic to think of these meals as distinct "eucharistic meals" separate from other community meals.[14] Moreover, the boundary between those with whom one could and could not eat are well patrolled in that the next comment in the *Didache* is: "Remember what the Lord has said about this: 'do not give to the dogs what is holy' " (9:5).[15] This implies a world of holy and common, clean and unclean, insiders and outsiders.[16] This is the precise set of assumptions among

12. This is not to assert that Luke knew the *Didache* in the form we have it—though that is not impossible—but merely to point out that the practices that Luke's story assumes as commonplace in early communities have marked similarities to those evidenced in the *Didache*.

13. See Draper 2007.

14. See McGowan 1997 and 1999.

15. One might point to Matt 7:6 as the basis of the *Didache*'s statement, but this would be to conclude too hastily; all we can say is that the *Didache* and Matthew reflect a common tradition.

16. To see the force of the image of dogs, one must look at this catena of texts: *Didache* 9:5; Mark 7:27-28, with parallel Matt 15:26-27; Matt 7:6; Phil 3:2; and Rev

disciples of Jesus such as Peter and his Jerusalem accusers that the story in Acts 10–11 is meant to undermine as baseless. To many early communities—such as those represented by the *Didache*—eating with outsiders was still problematic, and something that could only take place after their repentance and baptism. Within the Lukan story we have the possibility that righteousness and the Spirit are there already, that God shows no partiality, and that no one is to be called unclean—and so, presumably not referred to as a "dog"—and so the final community is *established* in the act of communal eating.

What Does This Mean for Us Today?

To suggest that practices of the early churches are a "normative norm" for all subsequent Christian practice—despite the fact that this is a claim that most churches have frequently invoked in the past—is neither practical (for we cannot re-create the social world of the first centuries) nor theologically justified (for it would be tantamount to a biblical fundamentalism with all its problems and faults). On the other hand, given that Christians today continue to read texts such as Acts and to value them as their precious common memories means that we do not simply consign them to the past as prologue. In this case, I would propose a rather simple hermeneutic: given that we make sense of our present in retrospection and recollection, we look to the past as a kind of wondrous mirror—one where we sometimes find a reflection in concerns and patterns of behavior and sometimes we find a distinct lack of reflection. In each case, the action of approaching the mirror is important in that it allows us to evaluate our own discipleship within our own situation. It could be that we are acting in virtually the same way as those we read about in the past. And this very lack of difference is the problem because the external situation has changed, or it could be that we are struck by the differences and these call us to question again our own assumptions even when we have set great value on them.[17] It is in this latter manner that I suggest that contemporary concerns about sharing the eucharistic meal, and the boundaries that are so often applied to its sharing, may gain insight from looking at an earlier

---

22:15, in which dogs are representative of the Gentiles, those who are wicked, those who are not part of God's first choice, and outsiders.

17. For a fuller expression of this hermeneutic, see O'Loughlin 2010, 145–60.

set of concerns about meal-sharing (and, as we have seen, this involved what we would call eucharistic meal-sharing) and boundaries. The earlier practice is not being presented as "this is what it should be" but rather as posing a set of important questions for today. These questions have a right to be considered in both theology and practice precisely because these memories, contained in Acts, are still today part of the formal memory of churches. These memories are part of our present as we recall them as part of our canon and read them in our gatherings. Hence that memory of meal-sharing and boundaries can be a meaningful part of any contemporary discussion of eucharistic sharing and boundaries.

So it is possible to look at meal practice in the churches then and today and see how they relate to and reflect one another; and that is the process that beckons us now if the case of Acts 10–11 is seen within this then-now process of reflection. Whatever way one responds to that reflection, it is always interesting to bring to attention alterative ancient views of matters that concern us, especially when they come from such figures of authority as an evangelist or from a text that is claimed unambiguously as part of the canon or from a memory that is directly linked to no less a figure than the apostle Peter. At the very least, to those who hold that their position is unalterable because of its grounding in tradition, history can provide a counter-indicative fact that undermines any claim to doctrinal unanimity on a matter! So what do we see in Acts 10–11? Simply this: eating together at a common table is basic not only to the baptized but to all humans who fear God (10:2). Eating together cannot just be seen as celebrating the bonds of the ecumenical—in both senses of the term—community of the risen Christ, but is part of the process by which this community is bought into being in the actual historical situations in which disciples find themselves. Moreover, the welcome to outsiders to come and share our table is part of the invitation that the disciples of The Way offer to all human beings who seek God and act uprightly. And, as part of our Christian memory this story does not claim apostolic authority, but as Luke relates it with visions and voices, it claims to be part of a specific revelation of God to the church so that it could fulfil its mission of witnessing out to the end of the earth (Acts 1:8; 13:47). Our memory serves as a call to churches that do not practice inter-Christian commensality to ask themselves whether they need to rethink in the light of the gospel—that is, the revealed good news which we proclaim—what is the fuller significance of Christian sharing at table.

We must never forget the fundamentals of our kerugma. The Lord is infinitely generous. God is the uniquely affluent giver of all that is good.[18] God is the God of infinite welcome: hence all boundaries are porous. Our boundaries, therefore, should reflect this and make space for anyone from beyond our borders at our banquets.

18. In the quotation with which this chapter began, Augustine calls God *largitor affluentissimus*.

6

Building upon Baptism

Baptism is participation in Christ's death and resurrection
(Rom 6:3-5; Col 2:12);
a washing away of sin (1 Cor 6:11);
a new birth (John 3:5);
an enlightenment by Christ (Eph 5:14);
a re-clothing in Christ (Gal 3:27);
a renewal by the Spirit (Titus 3:5);
the experience of salvation from the flood (1 Pet 3:20-21);
an exodus from bondage (1 Cor 10:1-2);
and a liberation into a new humanity in which barriers of
division whether of sex or race or social status are transcended
(Gal 3:27-28; 1 Cor 12:13).
The images are many but the reality is one.
—BEM[1]

There seems to be one event in the Christian's life upon which there is widespread agreement: baptism. Because in the received text of the Bible (in Matt 28:19) there is a clear mandate to perform this ritual and apparently guidance on its performance, it has largely escaped being the subject of controversy since the sixteenth century. Moreover, it is widely agreed that one becomes a Christian through baptism and that every denomination that practices baptism is a community of genuine Christians. So it is baptism—the sacrament that is common across the churches—that

1. *Baptism, Eucharist and Ministry*, 1982, Baptism, II, 2.

should be the basis for ecumenical progress.[2] And, if there is a theological basis for intercommunion, then this should be based "on our common baptism." This appeal to baptism can be seen in the reply Pope Francis made to Anke de Bernardinis in 2015. Having already mentioned baptism twice in his answer, the Pope said:

> Always make reference to Baptism: "One faith, one Baptism, one Lord," so Paul says to us, and from there take the consequences.[3]

Faced with Pope Francis's statement, backed up by an early Christian slogan "One Lord, one faith, one baptism" (Eph 4:5), which the pope cites with the traditional ascription to Paul, many people wonder why there is any problem at all with non-Catholics sharing at our table. If the eucharist is the meal of the Christians, and it is baptism that makes one a Christian, so then should not every Christian share in this meal? The logic seems crisp and clear, so where is the problem? The problem is that while our understanding of baptism appears to be unproblematic, virtually every statement that I made in the opening paragraph of this chapter is, or has been, controversial. Some of those statements are now only problematic for some churches (the classic example is whether an infant can be baptized or whether only a believer?). But, every church, including our own, has problems about both the practice (e.g., should you baptize an infant when the parents are only culturally Christian?) or meaning (e.g., is it about "washing away" original sin or beginning a new life—and, what do we mean by "original sin" anyway if we preach neither Limbo nor God damning the unbaptized) of baptism?

This problem is further complicated by the fact that most Catholics today imagine that their understanding of baptism is simple and straightforward. Unfortunately, it is, in fact, so often based on such a narrow perception of baptism—derived, on the whole, more from canonical practice than theological reflection[4]—that while it is broad enough to allow us to see that someone who is a member of another church is truly a Christian, it is not so embracing an understanding of baptism as to allow us to see other Christians as having the same access to the table as a fellow Catholic. There-

2. Formally expressed in the Vatican's 1970 document: "Reflections and Suggestions Concerning Ecumenical Dialogue" III, 1 in Flannery 1975, 541.

3. See chapter 1 above.

4. See O'Loughlin 2017.

fore, if we want to pick up the pope's challenge to investigate the theology underlying intercommunion and, in doing so, "make reference to baptism" as he asks, then we need to look first at some of our common ideas about baptism and ask whether we need a richer theology of baptism.

Doorway to the Sacraments

I was eight years old when I learned this phrase in school. It was a way of giving a one-line answer to the question of why baptism is important. It was significant, because without it one could not receive the other sacraments—such as Holy Communion—and with them God's grace. Baptism was something like a cinema ticket that had to be presented at the door before one was allowed to take one's place in the auditorium and then sit down and enjoy the film. As with all such entry tickets, it was something that one passed beyond. One had to go through it—though this was taken care of for me by my parents when I was just ten days old—and had to be able to prove that one had been baptized (by getting a copy of one's baptismal certificate), but in reality it was over and done with. Having got the necessary "tick in the box," I could now move on with a being a Christian.

Baptism was also necessary for an even more important reason: without it, a child who died would be deprived of the full joy of heaven and be, forever, hovering on heaven's threshold (popularly referred to as being in limbo) or even worse. By the time I was growing up in the early 1960s the older off-the-cuff teaching that those who died without baptism faced damnation had disappeared, and teachers had to juggle two apparently contradictory statements before their class: first, "baptism was necessary for salvation," and second, "not all the unbaptized are damned." Rather than challenging the application of such categorical logic to a transcendent subject, indeed a mystery, most teachers wanted to keep the seeming clarity and so had recourse to a wider image of baptism such that it embraced baptism of water (those baptized in the usual way), baptism of blood' (those who suffered for goodness and truth but did not know the gospel), and baptism of desire (those who, through no fault of their own, never heard the gospel but lived good lives). If we leave aside the inadequacy of this approach's vision of a god of vengeance when compared with the God preached by Jesus who is the Father superabundant in his loving and giving, we might note one common element with the doorway approach: once again baptism is a matter of dealing with the past. This views baptism as the remedy for an inherited fault that leads to death, and once that danger has been removed (when original sin is washed away and finished with), then baptism has done its work. So, problem solved (I have been baptized), and I can then forget about that problem and move on to new things and fresh problems.

One might point out now that most preachers have not preached in this way for decades, nor has any official catechism promoted these views, and we have had a new liturgy since 1969, and many Catholic communities have embraced a more integrated form of initiation. It always pleases me when I hear a group use the abbreviation RCIA with as much ease as TV—but that does not mean that the older ideas are not there in our collective memory and in a broad cultural memory invigorated by such ideas in common chatter and rekindled by cultural superstitions. Is there a parish where a child of two or three has not been presented for baptism by parents with only a very tenuous relationship to the church, and it turns out that a grandaunt has told them that the baby has been sick because "the sin is still in it" and baptism will work like an antibiotic?! Such ideas are deeper set in our depths than we often like to admit.

Baptism was, and is, unusual in another way. Of the seven rituals that Catholics set in a special category, the seven sacraments, marriage and baptism stand apart because they do not *need* a priest as minister. While all seven usually have a priest involved in some way, in marriage the couple are the ministers and the priest is there as a witness,[5] and anyone can baptize someone and, in terms of effects, it is "just as good" as if the pope himself performed the baptism. Indeed, look at any older Catholic prayer book and you will find in an obvious place in big letters a notice like this:

LAY BAPTISM

Any person, whether man, woman, or child, may baptize an infant in danger of death, and ought to do so, without waiting to send for a Priest.
Take common water, pour it on the head or face of the child and while pouring it say: "I baptize thee in the name of the Father, and of the Son, and of the Holy Ghost."

5. A canonist would not find this adequate, but it will serve as a shorthand: this is not a book on the seven sacraments, much less on marriage.

While this sign highlighted the importance of baptism in a dramatic way, it also sent out another signal: baptism was a once-off moment, it only was to be thought of in terms of salvation *post-mortem*, and, indeed, it was so basic that anyone could give it. It did not need valid orders, it did not need the sanction of the church [that is, the ecclesiastical structures], and it was but the minimal entry level to being a Christian.

Another consequence of this way of thinking is that "our common baptism" is reduced to being actually quite a small event: just the bare entry level that puts you under the "Christian" banner. Indeed, it is not seen as a positive quality in the other but rather merely something they could not lose (since it did not need valid orders). Baptism, far from being our common boast, was but a fact that they did not lose everything and, indeed, on the basis of *our* canonical approach to the sacraments *they* could be said to have received it. If that is how one views baptism, then it is hardly enough upon which to base any argument in favor of intercommunion: all it says is that they are not wholly outside the Christian fold as a result of their theological decisions in the sixteenth century, and that we can talk to them. It is this view of baptism as a once-off canonical event that underpins much of the reasoning that sees the need for some other, higher level of ecclesial communion as necessary before we could have not only fellowship in the name "Christian" but at the table. While many Catholics will now object that this is not what we officially teach (and I would agree), we should note that this view is still very much an operative theology. This was brought home to me in a discussion among theologians after the publication in 1998 of *One Bread One Body* (which argued that there was need for much greater communion than that founded on baptism if there was to be intercommunion), when it was suggested that the document did not pay sufficient attention to what we understand to be the effects of baptism, and eventually a spokesman for the bishops declared, with exasperation, that "Baptism is not the answer to any of our problems. Everyone has baptism." In the light of that comment I just fell silent: if everyone had baptism and baptism was a living reality in everyone, then what a wonderful state the church would be in!

Pope Francis stressed that we had to make reference to baptism: it could be that he was somehow aware that if we had a more adequate understanding of baptism, then the problems about sharing in the eucharist would be put in a completely different light. All great changes begin with a new understanding, and perhaps before we can be happy to share with other Christians we need a new way of thinking about, appreciating, and being thankful for baptism?

Once-off or Ongoing?

That baptism is not simply a remedy for original sin or an entry ticket to the church has always been recognized in some way or other. Even the notion of the doorway assumed that one was going to continue on to celebrate other sacraments. Moreover, it was widely presented that baptism was a disposition within the person such that they could receive further graces. Aquinas famously developed this line of thinking. Starting with the practice that baptism was unrepeatable—a fact of Christian practice that had long been explained by the notion that baptism has imprinted a character that may not be erased—Thomas asked about the nature of this character and saw it as an ability given to us to receive the ability from God to engage in divine worship. This was, in baptism, a passive ability (*potentia passiva*) such that one could take part in worship and this would be fruitful for the person.[6] He then went on to argue that the imprint gave a shape to the person and this shape was distinctly Christlike. It makes the person fit for the enjoyment of glory and

> each faithful Christian is marked out [by the character] to receive or to hand on to others what is linked to the worship of God. . . . Now our Christian rituals are, taken together, derived from the priesthood of the Christ, and so it is plainly the case that the sacramental character is in a special way Christ-shaped because by the character the Christians are shaped to his priesthood. These characters [of baptism, confirmation, and order] are, indeed, nothing other than, in some way, participations in the Christ's priesthood and derive from the Christ himself.[7]

This is quite an amazing passage in comparison with the common operative theology of baptism to which we so readily default. Thomas is making the case for an ongoing dimension of baptism (character) that links us to the Christ, now our intercessor as priest with the Father, such that we can take a full part in the life of the liturgy. Furthermore, while

6. Thomas Aquinas, *Summa theologiae* III, q. 63, a. 2, co.
7. Thomas Aquinas, *Summa theologiae* III, q. 63, a. 3, co.

he distinguishes kinds of characters and in this employs the notion of "active" and "passive" abilities (*potentiae*), he sees the ability to participate in worship as given to each member of the faithful (*quisque fidelis*). Baptism's character is what makes you a liturgical actor.

Thomas Aquinas (1225–74) never had to think about the issue of intercommunion. In his time there appeared to be, in the Latin West, just a single church, and anyone who sought to distance him or herself from that church (and there were such groups) would have wanted minimal contact with Catholics. The more significant is that in his time most people only received communion very rarely: usually only once a year. While ordinary Christians (i.e., non-clerics) were expected to attend (literally: "listen" or "hear") Mass on Sundays, it would have been seen as most exceptional for them to have "gone to communion." Indeed, so infrequent was eating at the meal (pardon the anachronistic language) that in 1215 the Fourth Lateran Council could decree that laypeople should "reverently receive the sacrament of the Eucharist at least at Easter unless they think, for a good reason and on the advice of their own priest, that they should abstain from receiving it for a time."[8] But on the basis of how he viewed the baptismal "character" we can sketch out an answer.

Each baptized person has been given by God a power to receive the gifts that belong to Christian worship, and like all God's gifts this comes without strings. It is a power that belongs to the person and using it is part of their fitting in with their status as baptized individuals. So one cannot hold this view of baptism—which is what empowers Catholics to take part in a eucharistic action—and then impose a ban on the person who in virtue of their baptism wishes to participate in the liturgy that involves eating by eating. Moreover, since the ongoing active ingredient of baptism is this character, and every baptized person has this, there are simply no visitors. Anyone baptized who is there is there by right, and all are on the same terms. With no visitors, each is a member of the family and has been enabled by the Father to take their place. Each is receiving the banquet from all, and each is contributing so that it is the banquet for all.

Now imagine this scene. A presbyter sees in the gathering a husband who was baptized a Catholic and a wife who was baptized a member of an evangelical church and who feels that that is her home church. She

8. Denzinger 812 (see Fastiggi and Englund Nash 2012, 271).

comes to the table to eat, and the presider is torn about what to do. If he gives her a share of the loaf, then he believes that he is doing something that is functionally forbidden, and he also feels that somehow there is an improper crossing of boundaries (and we as humans love to have boundaries of belonging: we build more walls in our minds every day than a bricklayer in a week). On the other hand, if he refuses her, he knows that it will cause scandal and hurt (and he somehow knows that letting a sacrament be the means for causing human hurt is somehow crazy) and will probably mean a whole family will depart from the Catholic Church. So, with doubts remaining, he administers communion to this outsider. The challenge for this presbyter is to see this character that is imprinted on both the husband and the wife, and indeed on himself. Each person is different, but all three have this common imprint that makes each of them shaped so as to be part of the priesthood of the Anointed One. Each is able to take part in the exchange that is the liturgy because of this common element. It is because all three have something in common that they are together and able to give thanks to the Father in the Christ. Seeing this shared shape, he should rejoice that the fact of each being there is a direct response to the Christ. So that woman's place at communion comes directly from the Lord. Her presence is true and proper; it is not to be thought of as simply a consequence of some formula in canon law that says she has gotten over a threshold.

If we take what Aquinas says about character seriously, then all the baptized who stand around the table stand there in the Christ. All are there because they have been given a share in his unique priesthood, which allows them to offer worship to the Father. As worshipers of the Father, they stand as sisters and brothers.

Conformity to the Risen Lord

The value of Aquinas's approach should not be downplayed. The *Summa* was written not to provide a great overarching theoretical narrative but as a guide for training young preachers and from which they could derive practical guidance for the new urban Christians of the thirteenth century.[9] And we may easily extract a pastoral sound bite from his treatment of

9. See Boyle 1982.

the long-term dimension of baptism: baptism is the empowerment of each to take part in the liturgy. However, that treatment was framed within the mental landscape of another world and employs the scholastic form of reasoning that, for us, creates as many problems as it solves. Where Aquinas tended to view questions in terms of dependencies (*x* depends on *y*, so *x* is secondary to *y*)—in the jargon this was known as causality—we find that we speak of matters of faith in terms of relationships and the meaning of those relationships. It is, indeed, just in such terms of relationship that we present baptism today within the liturgy.

At baptism, among many other things, I am making a commitment to discipleship, an explicit statement that I am responding to the work of the Spirit within my being and that this will shape the way I live. But discipleship is not something I do alone; it is being part of a community. The Father has formed a community of his covenant in Jesus the Anointed One, and I have entered into a relationship with the Father and with his community. This community has many names. To outsiders it is an ideological party or a religious fan club: the Christians. To insiders who take part in a local gathering, a church, it takes a name from the collection of those gathering: the church. When it reflects on how it is called to behave, it becomes The Way, and when it wants to designate its relationship to its divine source it calls itself the people of God. At each and every turn it is a set of relationships of sisters and brothers in the Christ, daughters and sons of the Father. Baptism is not just a ritual moment but the reality of the relationship between us, and between us and God. We cannot be together as a church apart from that relationship, and if we are together because of that relationship, then this has primacy in all we do.

There will always be all sorts of problems in our actual relationships within the church and in each local church because human beings are factious animals, but how do these disputes relate to baptism? Our baptismal relationship to one another and the Father abides within us like a covenant: if you are willing to come among us, then we have to recognize that fundamental relationship and not let disagreements occlude it. Likewise, if I enter a community of the baptized, my baptismal relationship with the Father means that I must acknowledge my baptismal relationship with those around me. In both cases, each one of us must be true to the fullness of what it means to call God our Father in the midst of the church. The relationships are what we must focus upon—eating and drinking together flow directly from this set of relationships. We should still sort out our differences, remove everything that is preventing our growth as individuals and as communities, strive for ever-greater unity of minds and hands and hearts, but in the meantime be thankful for God's covenant extended in baptism. That covenantal love is always greater than our disputes.

Affirming Baptism

There is a curious lack of symmetry in the ways we approach the catechesis of baptism and the eucharist. Over the past century there have been umpteen projects and campaigns to help Catholics deepen and renew both their approach to the eucharist and their appreciation of what they are doing when they gather for it. More quietly, but just as insistently, there have been projects that sought to remove superstitions surrounding the eucharist and false teaching about it. This is an ongoing task. By contrast, we have not given nearly as much emphasis to renewing our general understanding of baptism (in spite of great efforts to introduce RCIA). But I suspect that the answer to many of our difficulties over sharing with other Christians at the Lord's table would diminish almost to a vanishing point if we renewed our vision of what we share as a result of having been through the Lord's bath. We have all been buried with Christ in this "plunging" and raised with him (Col 2:12), and so it is as the new, raised up people that we stand around the table. To then tell one standing there that they cannot eat or drink at that table amounts to denying that that person is one of the New People who have put on Christ in baptism (Gal 3:27).

We need to imagine baptism not as an event but as an ongoing presence. "I am one of the baptized now" rather than "I was baptized." It is this vision of baptism as a constant state, baptism as the reality that we call discipleship, that I hear in the pope's comments to Anke de Bernardinis's question. He began:

> Don't we have the same Baptism? And if we have the same Baptism, we must walk together.

Baptism is not just the beginning of the journey, it is the journey itself. It is something we have now, and it determines our walking together now. This is further developed in his second comment, which presents a continuing baptism as part of the journey of individuals within their community:

> We have the same Baptism. When you feel yourself a sinner—I also feel myself very much a sinner—when your husband feels himself a sinner, you go before the Lord and ask for forgiveness; your husband does the same and goes to the priest and asks for absolution. They are remedies to keep Baptism alive. When you pray together, that Baptism grows, it becomes strong; when you teach your children who Jesus is, why Jesus came, what Jesus did for us, do the same, be it in Lutheran language or in Catholic language, but it's the same.

Baptism is not just simply there, much less a past event, but is something that grows. I need to grow my baptism in the immediate surroundings of my life; I need to act in such a way that I help baptism to grow in those disciples with whom I live. Indeed, I can use this notion—my helping baptism to grow in those around me—as a rule of thumb for my own Christian behavior. So at a eucharistic gathering do I see a Methodist or a Presbyterian, or do I see a baptized sister or a baptized brother? When I recall my duty to help us all to grow in baptism, then only a complete and fulsome welcome at the table is worthy of us because there is but "one Lord, one faith, one baptism" (Eph 4:5).

Appendix: Living in a Global Situation

This chapter has focused on the basic role of baptism in relationship to the eucharist. As such, it is in line with the main purpose of this book, which is to explore if there are theological grounds for a change in the Roman Catholic Church's practical position on admitting other Christians to sharing in the eucharist while remaining members of their own churches. However, many will have wondered if there is not a deeper question here that must be addressed: What of those people of good will (see Luke 2:14) who are not baptized and who are present at a eucharistic gathering of Christians?

This issue receives almost no formal discussion within the Catholic Church, but it is a real pastoral issue where there are often family members present at a eucharist who, while they may not have any sense of formal faith, are also not simply interlopers on the gathering. Is it just a case that they should be told that only those who have been ritually baptized—we must be careful not to identify the baptized with those who have been part of an explicit Christian ritual—can take part and that everyone else must see her/himself as an outsider? While this answer has a long history within Christian practice, arguably already found in the *Didache*,[10] it seems to many that this is hardly the reception that they would expect Jesus to give to such a person who happens to find her/himself at his table. Moreover, while few would use the ancient metaphor of "giving the children's food to the dogs," many feel that anything that amounts to an outright refusal is hardly conducive to the church's vocation to help all to move toward discipleship.

To examine this question adequately is beyond the scope of this present book, but also it would be fatuous not to acknowledge that this is a real pastoral problem that requires creative theological thinking rather than simple repetitions of inherited formulae. It is also a case where there is scope for receptive ecumenism: learning from other churches and benefiting from their experience.

One source from which we can learn is the Episcopal parish of St. Gregory of Nyssa in San Francisco. For some years past that community has been practicing just such "open to all" eucharistic hospitality and has been doing so with what is by now a well-developed theological underpinning and with a liturgy crafted to emphasize the universal welcome of the Christ. This, in turn, has prompted a discussion among Episcopal theologians and liturgists that has shown some of the problems of the inherited position and of the pastoral complexity of the missionary aspect of our vocation in our multicultural situation. It is worth looking at the worship book of St. Gregory of Nyssa parish (*Celebrating the Eucharist with St. Gregory of Nyssa Episcopal Church*[11]) and at some of the papers that it has generated in academic journals.[12]

10. *Didache* 9:5 reads: "Only let those who have been baptised in the name of the Lord eat and drink at your eucharists. And remember what the Lord has said about this: do not give to dogs what is holy." On the possible meaning of this rule in the *Didache*, see Van de Sandt 2002; on its pastoral application today, see Bates 2005.

11. See www.saintgregorys.org (accessed February 14, 2018).

12. This is a selection, in chronological order, that sets out the debate and some of the developments that have arisen from the debate: Farwell 2004; Tanner 2004; Farwell 2005; Phillips 2005; Bates 2005; Edmonson 2009; Meyers 2012; and Schell 2012.

Given that Catholics still energetically guard the fence they place around the eucharist, it might seem silly to even raise the question of more open hospitality or, at least, not politically wise to do so—as if even discussing this issue would further harden Catholic attitudes to Christian intercommunion. However, in a secular age where religious belonging is perceived as being "just another option" in a manner that previous human generations could never have imagined, this is a pressing question that challenges not only our pastoral responses but our theological assumptions. The actual presence at our gatherings of those who are not baptized is a pastoral concern that cannot be ignored, and anyone doing so must not see it as simply a matter of applying a law but be mindful that there is a higher law of pastoral responsibility: *salus animarum suprema lex*,[13] and the pastor must care for every human sister or brother with whom he comes into contact and not only those who are brothers or sisters in the Christ. What, for example, is the effect on such a guest to be told, following the surest warrants of antiquity, that for that guest to be acknowledged at the table would be equivalent to giving our food to the dog? If that person's journey toward God is hampered by such an action—and the eucharist is (whatever else it is) always a human action, an event in the human sphere—then one must not do it.

But, for now, it is sufficient to note that the topic of this book, Christian intercommunion, will open onto larger issues relating to pastoral challenges of mission, evangelization, and initiation.

13. The principle of canonical interpretation, *salus animarum suprema lex*, is not restricted in its application to those who are visibly members of the church.

7

The Eucharist and the Pilgrims' Journey

I wonder:
is the sharing of the Lord's Supper the end *of a journey*
or the viaticum *to journey together?*
I leave the question to the theologians, to those who understand.
—Pope Francis

The question with which this book is concerned—who can share at the eucharistic table—is not a new one. Since at least the middle of the third century, this issue has been at the center of theological reflection on pastoral practice. Then, in the aftermath of the Decian Persecution, the crucial question was whether someone who had survived the persecution by avoiding saying "I am a Christian" could be forgiven and once more share in the eucharistic meal. Indeed, the whole history of the eucharist (as distinct from the history of its liturgical development) can be narrated as different answers to "Who can eat (and drink) at the eucharist?" However, in contrast to the period since around the beginning of the twentieth century when, very gradually, there were moves get more participants to eat, the dominant theme in Christian history has been to find out how *few* of those present should eat and drink, and to set out very clearly the criteria by which Christians should be either permanently or temporarily excluded from the table.

Running down the centuries we have two conflicting streams in both preaching and praxis. On one side, we have a constant stress on the eucharist being the food for Christians, that which is given to them to eat and to support them on their journey. But simultaneously we have a fearful insistence, usually hedged about with some vague threat, that only those who have met certain stringent conditions can actually avail of that food.

The repetition of the theme of Christians' need to eat of this food comes mainly from the liturgy itself. First and foremost, we have the *fact* of the liturgy itself. The eucharistic liturgy has a meal-shape—to say the very least—and this supposes the occasion for the gathering, which is the offering linked to bread and wine upon a table, is to be considered significant for those for whom these are being offered. Second, within the language of the liturgy—at least since the time that the so-called "institution narrative" became part of the text of the Eucharistic Prayer[1]—are explicit statements about taking and eating and drinking. Third, there are the images that have been used in praise of the eucharist such as the text from the psalms "he fed them with the finest wheat" (*Cibavit eos*)[2] or antiphons such as "O sacred banquet"[3] which, in turn, have become musical features on their own that describe the liturgy. Meanwhile, in preaching there have been the use of themes from John 6 and the bread of life, while in painting the Last Supper image became the archetype for the eucharistic gathering.

However, this theme of the eucharist as food came mainly in the softer register of the poetry of the liturgy or the reflective metaphors of the homilist. In any case, only a very few people had such access to the liturgy as to perceive this theme: walls of stone, grilles of wood and iron, and barriers of language, education, and silence meant that if you heard and understood these words and signs, you were probably a cleric of some sort.

On the other hand, there were some very definite obstacles to linking the eucharist with everyday life, its sustenance, and such an earthy business as eating. The ritual surrounding the ritual inhibited any link between our spiritual needs and this gift. So the keeping of the fasting regulations became so important that eating (and drinking) became a function of them. Fasting not only discouraged participation directly (on the one day many could rest) but created a sense of scrupulosity: as recently as the 1950s, seminarians were being taught to set the minds of

1. The insertion of the memorial of the words of Jesus within the anaphora was a later development; see Taft 2003.

2. Ps 80:17.

3. From the liturgy of Corpus Christi.

those who had swallowed snow flakes on their way to Mass (when they had prepared to go to communion by going to confession) at rest, but then added to the development of such scruples by saying "provided it was accidental and that people should try to keep their mouths closed"! Moreover, fasting was regulated in terms of food and drink, but was invariably taken to include sexual intercourse between husbands and wives. Again, seminarians in the 1950s were told to set the scruples of the pious at rest, but this took a perverse form: it was not sinful to receive communion after coition, and without having been to confession, but you could choose to abstain from receiving out of respect. Meanwhile, in some places, for a young married man to take communion was to leave himself open to ridicule from his fellows, for the world divided into two camps: the communicants and the sexual achievers. Likewise, there were very clear statements about who could not, under any circumstances, receive communion: anyone in an irregular sexual union. This has survived to this day in the regulations on the divorced and remarried, which are often seen as the very headline preaching of the church on the eucharist. While there was a vast body of scholarship on the exceptions to this rule, and a secondary body of work on how any doubt about the exception applied, for most people it was a black and white situation: unless you were absolutely sure you were "safe" to receive, it was better to stay away. It was the legacy of this fear that led to the practice in the twentieth century, when the liturgical movement began advocating regular Sunday communion, of arguing that there was need for confession on the previous evening. Until the twentieth century frequent confession was far less often mentioned because on an average Sunday (even at the early Mass, when most who were going to communion would attend) perhaps one or two people would receive. In that case, they would tell the priest beforehand as an additional rite had to be added to the 1570 liturgy if it were found that someone did want to receive at Mass.[4] Moreover, this dissociation of the eucharist with eating and drinking cohered well with the dominant

4. The 1570 missal contained a ritual for communion of the people that was not an intrinsic part of the rite, and this is sometimes explained as simply an error whereby a text intended for a priest celebrating a *missa privata* was adopted as the standard text. But this was not a slip: the *de facto* standard was the *missa privata*—the server was not normally given communion—and so this was adopted as the *de iure* standard.

eucharistic spirituality. Since the sixth century in the West, the liturgy was presented in terms of a rereading of the Jerusalem temple liturgy and so stressed the notion of the otherworldliness, the sublime wonder of the "most blessed (*sacrosanctissimum*) sacrament," and of the unworthiness of those present to come close to the divine presence. Just as the Holy of Holies was bounded by barrier after barrier that stressed the degrees of holiness, and thereby the separation of the Holy from the creation, so the eucharist became the Christian *ganz andere* in "the tabernacle"—and note this is a temple-related word. Since anyone who recalled the principle *sacramenta propter homines* (sacraments belong within the human world) was liable to be accused of denying the real presence—note that "presence" is another temple-based concept—few sought to extend the theology of eucharist beyond "the sanctuary"—except in such ways as the annual Corpus Christi procession.

Whereas the theme of the eucharist as food was relatively unseen and framed in the language of symbols, the theme of the eucharist as that which was somehow beyond the ambience of the ordinary Christian was boldly announced in firm language of law backed up by warnings of the penalties for unworthy reception. Indeed, the whole emphasis shifted from "Who is positively excluded?" to deciding how few were actually allowed to receive: unless you could show you could receive, the presumption was that you should not and would not.[5]

The Unacknowledged Legacy

Looking back on past Catholic attitudes to eating and drinking at the eucharist might seem far from approaching the question of intercom-

5. These sorts of negative sifting tools can be hard to think through as we tend to change them into positives. So consider this parallel: you are the teacher about to grade the essays of an entire cohort of students; you can presume that since they are in your class they are capable of completing the essay, and so it is the exception who fails (this equates the case of the expectation that Christians eat at the eucharist unless inhibited from doing so). Now contrast the person compiling a shortlist to find a replacement teacher, bringing a sizable group of applicants down to manageable proportions. This person begins by triage, assuming that the applications will be removed unless there is something specific that merits a second look (this equates to the case that you expect no one to take communion unless there is positive evidence that they should).

munion between various churches going forward. However, we need to consider our past in detail because we Catholics are so accustomed to certain mental habits that we find ourselves considering the act of eating at the eucharist negatively. We start from the idea that someone cannot "receive" communion unless they meet certain requirements. In other words, you are excluded unless you pass a test: eating at the eucharist is not simply part of being a Christian. So underneath the whole question of viewing the eucharist as *viaticum* lies the question of "the benefit of the doubt" and whether eating is a normal part of the pilgrim life of disciples. The choice is between (a) should we presume eating unless there is a known problem, and (b) should we presume non-eating unless we have a definite indicator that one could eat. In our everyday preaching we have, since the Second Vatican Council, moved decisively toward the first option, but we are still so familiar with the language of the second option and the situations that arise from it that we slip back into that form of decision-making without realizing it.

But why is this question important for the future? The effect of eating at the eucharist becoming the exception rather than the rule—indeed the rare exception—brought about a very fundamental shift in the way we related reception of the eucharist to the living of the Christian life. We saw in the previous chapter the rule promulgated by the Fourth Lateran Council in 1215. Under fear of penalty, each adult Christian (that is, Latin Christian) was to go to communion once a year at Eastertime.[6] In order to make this annual communion (something that was more frequent than was common in many places), the person had to go to confession, and even then there was an allowance that one could still abstain if the confessor thought such abstinence justified. We might counter with the question as to why Jesus introduced the idea of eating and drinking if it could be better for one's spiritual health not to do as he said, but that would fail to take account of the situation. For centuries, reception of the eucharist had been linked with being free from sin; so the question in their minds was whether one could be so free of sin that one could worthily receive. The only way to ensure this was confession. This thinking has survived in various ways until our own time: going to communion is somehow a statement of worthiness, while the fact that we still have "Easter Duty"

6. Denzinger 812 (see Fastiggi and Englund Nash 2012, 271); and see ch. 6 above.

as part of our canon law[7] along with concerns of "consciousness of grave sin"[8] means that we revisit, time and again, the medieval perception.

If you must be virtually free from sin to receive communion, then that reception is *not* part of the struggle of the Christian life, but rather its end. The reception of the eucharist becomes, in itself, the goal of the Christian life—and if you are just struggling toward that goal of Christian living, and conscious of your own failures in living a good life, then you stay away. You go to Mass but do not imagine that you are in a fit state to fully take part. The reception of the eucharist is, *de facto*, a reward for the pious. We now speak of the eucharist as the summit of the Christian life, but should note that if the summit is imagined as a goal—just as the mountaineer might say "the summit is my goal"—then who in their right mind can say that there is not room for improvement? This is the logical and theological conundrum that afflicted Arnauld in the seventeenth century: he wanted to write a book advocating frequent communion and ended up arguing how infrequent it should be![9]

This vision of the eucharist as the aim toward which we strive was then reinforced by a range of practices, each explicable in itself, which served to say to us that receiving the eucharist is a goal of perfection, a reward for righteousness,[10] and somehow commensurate with worthiness. The cup was, for as long as any could remember, reserved to the celebrant, which meant that there were degrees of access all through the practice: from communion with just the eyes at the elevation to communion in "the species of bread" occasionally for the laity, and to receiving the cup which the priest, in virtue of his ontological otherness and duty, had to receive. The focus of the cult was upon the presence of the species so one entered into a relationship with the Lord in the eucharist in benediction, exposition, and through the eyes, while the corresponding focus in forming a spirituality of the eucharist was upon "making a spiritual communion" since the communion of actually eating was already precluded. As such the eucharist became not only an *end* (*telos*) for the Christian,

7. Canon 920 (1983 Code).

8. Canon 916 (1983 Code).

9. Antoine Arnauld (1612–94) published his *De la fréquente communion* in 1643.

10. It was this aspect of the eucharist—that it was the reward for righteousness as a result of the efforts of the individual—that was one of the fundamental causes of the splitting of the Western church in the sixteenth century; see Wandel 2006.

but the form of the very end of the Christian life in that a sacrament (by definition a *means*) became identified with the very "End"[11] of Christian faith in that it was the subject of adoration. This way of relating to the eucharist could be seen most explicitly in the cult of eucharistic adoration and can still be seen in the frequency with which hymns composed for adoration (such as "O Sacrament Most Holy") are still used around the time of communion in the reformed rite of Vatican II. Meanwhile, the separation of "Mass" and "Communion" as, in effect, different realities for the majority of Catholics was a visible fact: communion was an additional ritual, almost always from the tabernacle, and in the twentieth century when there were "crusades" for daily communion it was often the case that communion was distributed *before* Mass from the tabernacle so as to save the priest time by having the additional ritual of "communion for the people" during Mass (and so delaying his own breakfast). We may have called much of the underlying theology of this whole religious world into question as a result of the Liturgical Movement and other advances in theology, but that does not mean we have worked out all the implications of this newer theology, nor learned in our practice to jettison past inadequacies. We are creatures of bodily memory and we tend to retain vestiges of the past cluttering our present rather than make clear breaks with our older selves.

There are three aspects of this older eucharistic culture at work in the current generally accepted Catholic practice regarding intercommunion, and they also underpin many of the documents issued by bishops' conferences on this issue. First, we discuss, apparently without any difficulty or sense that there is something not right, the notion that one can take part in a eucharist, really and fruitfully, without actually eating and drinking. This implicitly falls back on the widespread distinction between Mass and Communion. Similarly, it assumes that one can be a fit subject for, and capable of, spiritual communion with the Christ, yet it could still be acceptable to imagine that actual eating and drinking was somehow more than this and that such participation required passing some higher threshold of acceptability before the throne of grace. There is little conscious thinking through that it is the nature of the unified act that is the eucharist so that if one is there, and taking part, then one eats and drinks because

11. "End" in this chapter is to be seen as purpose in a fuller sense, not just the purpose of a particular rite but of the whole Christian life.

that is the nature of the activity.[12] And likewise, that if one is actually taking part *spiritually* in a sacramental encounter, then upon what basis is one to be excluded from the sacramental activities of the encounter, which in this case is eating and drinking? Second, if it is argued that one cannot have the sign of the unity of the church—taken to be eating and drinking—until the reality of that unity, then the actual eucharistic activity of the church is an "End" in itself such that all are actually unworthy of eating and drinking now. The only consistent position would be for all Christians (except for celebrants who must "consume the species" to effect the sacrament) to postpone eating until the End. This may seem an absurd conclusion in any matter relating to the sacramental life of Christians, but it was a conclusion arrived at in practice by Catholics—and many of the churches of the Reformation who on this matter took over much implicitly—for centuries. And third, that there is a demand for theological unity if non-Catholics are to eat and drink has echoes of the notion that it is only by fulfilling certain criteria of worthiness that one can so take part in the eucharist. Put another way, if one has not the correct theology, and so, *de facto*, the ecclesial manifestation of that incorrect theology, one is not a fit person for eating and drinking at our celebrations. Once again, one is approaching participation as that which one limits to those who pass a high bar of suitability (defaulting to a presumption of exclusion due to unworthiness or unsuitability). The converse would be to see any person's desire to be there and participate as a manifestation of common faith (that is, defaulting to a presumption of welcome).

Medicine for the Soul

While the notion of the eucharist as *viaticum* (literally: provision for the journey) is ancient, we should note that it has not been a dominant theme in our eucharistic practice or preaching. Already by 325—at the Council of Nicaea, which contains our earliest formal mention of the term—there was hesitancy about viewing reception of the eucharist as a normal part of the ongoing life of Christians. Nicaea's thirteenth canon is anxious to reaffirm "the ancient rule" that the dying should not be denied the *viaticum* (*ephodion*) that they need. So the force of the law is that it expects

12. See ch. 2 above.

few to be eating at the eucharist and, indeed, that some clergy would not even admit the dying to the eucharist. That this very restrictive vision of eating at the eucharist underlies the law is then made explicit. The canon adds that if the person who is thought to be at death's door makes a recovery and is once again "numbered among the living," he shall only participate by prayer (that is, what more recent Catholic theology would call "spiritual communion"). Then Nicaea set out what it calls a general rule: "Should any dying person seek to share in the eucharist, the bishop after examining the case may give that person a share."[13] *Viaticum* would become not only the sacrament of the dying, but often—much to the annoyance of some such as Augustine—the only time that ordinary Christians ate of the eucharistic loaf.[14] This has had an enormous impact on our liturgy and perception. On the one hand, the reservation of the sacrament became a practice in response to this need to give communion to the dying;[15] while on the other, anyone who expressed a great desire to eat of the Lord's loaf was virtually admitting that they knew their death was imminent.[16]

Moreover, when any writer (such as John Cassian) or group (those who compiled the penitentials) took a therapeutic approach to the Christian life—that individuals on their journey need sustenance and medicine to support them—they did not advocate eating at the eucharist but the very opposite. The person seeking to repair the damage of sin should refrain (even if a monk) from the eucharist and use medicine to promote healing. However, this medicine was invariably a prescription for a specific combination of prayer, fasting, and almsgiving.[17]

There is one famous reference to the eucharist as medicine found in the prayer attributed to St. Thomas Aquinas that is still set forth in liturgical

13. Denzinger 129 (see Fastiggi and Englund Nash 2012, 53); the translation here is my own, and for the Latin text of Nicaea, upon which Western practice is based, see Alberigo 1962, 11.

14. There was an echo of this in the Roman rite until 1962, in that the priest about to give the communicant communion used the formula intended for the time just before death ("May the body of the Christ guard your soul until you reach eternal life"). In 1962 it was replaced with the formula now in use: "The Body of Christ."

15. See Freestone 1917, 3–16.

16. See O'Loughlin 2014a.

17. See Kursawa 2017.

books as one of the prayers that the celebrant may say as a preparation for Mass:[18]

> I approach the sacrament . . .
> as a sick man coming to the physician who will save his life,
> as an unclean man to the fountain of mercy,
> as a blind man to the radiance of eternal light,
> as one who is poor and needy before the Lord of heaven and earth
> while praying that your infinite generosity might,
> if you so will it,
> to cure my illness,
> wash away my filth,
> give light to my blind eyes,
> give abundance in my poverty and covering to my nakedness.

This explicitly presents the eucharist as sustenance, help, and support to a needy and incomplete pilgrim—and so can be seen to anticipate the modern liturgical movement's shift in emphasis from reward to support—but we should bear in mind that it was composed for use by a priest as part of his personal preparation for something which, out of the duty of his office, he had to do: to eat and drink at the table. So far from being a general vision of the place of the eucharist in the spiritual journey of Christians, this is focused on the spirituality of the celebrant. Moreover, it envisions the eucharist within the perspective of the pure contrasting with the impure, and it prays that the priest may be removed by grace from one state to the other. It is not a prayer for assistance in the actual motion of life amid its weaknesses, mess, and incompleteness. The same priest that recited this prayer kneeling on a sacristy priedieu would a few minutes later, on going up the steps to the altar for the first time during the liturgy, have prayed silently thus:

18. The Latin text can be found in most pre-1962 missals, and there is a translation at the back of each volume of the 1974 English edition of the Liturgy of the Hours in the section entitled "Preparation for Mass." These prayers were never compulsory but were highly recommended (see Murphy 1961, 59). In sacristies until the mid-1970s—and still in some places today—they were printed on special charts affixed to the wall and with a kneeler in front of them.

> Take from us, we beseech you, O Lord, our iniquities
> That, with pure minds, we might worthily enter
> the Holy of Holies,
> through Christ our Lord.[19]

These prayers belong to a vision of the eucharist as a sacral destination, set apart from lived experience, rather than one which understands a sacrament as an encounter along a journey.

When Pope Francis spoke about the shift from viewing the eucharist as the end of a journey to being support for the traveling, he was in line with a tradition of theology that can be traced for just over a century, but one that only reached the full light of day with Vatican II. However, that shift is a much larger task for us, as Catholics, to realize than is often imagined. Moreover, it is part of the reform of the liturgy that is called for out of the nature of the liturgy itself so that it can be more truly itself, rather than a development that is called for simply because it would facilitate ecumenical eating. The shift is not simply a shift in practice and its regulation, nor simply a change of theological outlook, but it is the challenge to move from one sacramental vision to another—and when one of these has been so deeply entrenched in our culture, such change is a veritable part of the conversion to which the gospel calls us (see Mark 1:15).

This change in vision from the eucharist as an end toward viewing it as a support for Christians on their life pilgrimage is something that should be a concern in and of itself. This is a key part of a movement of eucharistic restoration with the churches, and especially the Catholic Church, since the nineteenth century, and making this change is important quite apart from the ecumenical issues that are the focus of this book. Moreover, the need to make this fundamental shift in vision is by no means confined to the Catholic Church or even to the so-called "liturgical churches," be they eastern or western. It can often be heard from members of the churches of the Reformation that one reason why they celebrate eucharist so infrequently is because it is unpopular, as people feel unworthy to take communion or still hear 1 Corinthians 11:29 as if it were an absolute warning rather than Paul's rhetorical injunction to take care of fellow church members at their common eucharistic meal. Centuries of thinking about eating at the eucharist as the preserve of a spiritual elite

19. This is the prayer *Aufer a nobis*; on its use, see Murphy 1961, 72.

have left their mark on all of us: even upon those for whom the rejection of any such an elite is a basic premise. But once we do make that shift, then the case for removing limits for those who belong to other churches disappears. Each of us is in need of this support for the next step in our journey. To refuse to share it with someone is a sinful arrogation to oneself of that which is part of the divine care for the church; it is the equivalent in sphere of faith to not sharing one's food with the hungry. Likewise, to refuse to eat what is offered, as in the case of a Catholic taking part in another's eucharist, is an act of spiritual pride, equivalent to the assertion: "I do not need sustenance for my journey; I can go it alone." Both attitudes are failures to recognize the Christ in the situation actually before us—to see the Lord in the needy person (Matt 25:37) or to discern the body of the Lord in the assembly eating and drinking (1 Cor 11:29).

Food Is an Analogue of Food

Faced with these two sacramental visions, most people with a deep community memory of the eucharist as an end—and such memories are far more embodied than simply ideas in the mind because they have become part of us through repeated bodily activities as groups[20]—ask questions about the basis of this approach. These questions arise because the approach seems so distant from the familiar emphasis on presence focused on the elements and the reverential awe of the sacred presented within a symbol-system of word, objects, and actions that relate to a temple. The answer to this sincere question is complex. It must start with our understanding of the incarnation: the Lord has established his tabernacle in our midst (John 1:14) and so we have moved from a temple on some mountain to worship "in spirit and truth" in the midst of our daily lives (John 4:20-24) and it is we, the people of God, who are the living stones of this new temple (1 Pet 2:5). The presence has moved from the holy of holies to a human being, Jesus, and we have been joined to him. It is in our assembly that we encounter the divine presence, and, paradoxically, this new religion is radically secular: it is out in the ordinary world because the whole creation has been made a place where holiness may be encountered through the Logos entering into his creation in Jesus the Christ.

20. See Connerton 1989.

Likewise, we could point to the nature of sacramentality: it is in and through the created realities of our lives that we encounter God who, alone, is an End. All sacraments—and there are any number of them—of their nature belong to our time and there is an element of provisionality to them. A failure to recognize this "on the way" nature of that which links us to God runs the risk of confusing the means with the ends—but, as Paul observed, all the gifts will pass and only love, which is identical with God, will abide (1 Cor 13). The whole sacramental area belongs to the time that will pass, when we see in a mirror dimly, and as such every part of it should be seen as ordered toward supporting us on the journey. And in this movement "through corporeal things towards the incorporeal" (Augustine) or "through shadows and sketches toward the truth" (Newman), we confront each week what is offered to us by the Lord in the liturgy—and see this as *viaticum*. We view each encounter as that which can support us on the next step of the adventure. Each liturgical assembly is like a reviving stopover at a motel on a long road to a luxury suite at our holiday destination where we will settle down and enjoy our rest!

However, in the context of our eucharistic celebrations there is a far more direct illustration of the significance of this shift in sacramental vision that is intrinsic to the liturgy itself. Food, alimentation and hydration, is a constant of human life. And it is as a follow-on from this need that sharing meals has such a role at the heart of human culture. But every added significance that food and meals have for us can be traced back to that primary reality. Food has meaning for us (we would die without it) *before* it has any signification for us (signification in the sense of signs, meanings, metaphors, or sacramentalities). Before food is ever an analogue for something other than its own reality—such as "I am the bread of life" (John 6:35)—it already is valued, understood, and precious. This puts us in connection with reality and with the Source and End of reality: God the creator. It is here, virtually at the core of our being, that we can understand why thanksgiving for food and the satisfaction that it brings us in life is at the center of liturgy. Food is food. Food is for eating and sharing rather than to be used as a sign of something else to be stared upon. Food that sustains us is not a singular event in our lives but a constant day-to-day need. Food keeps us going, sustains us, and gives us joy.[21] It is with

21. The second blessing at a meal—in this case the blessing of the cup after supper—is a thanksgiving for the joy of the table, its sharing and eating. This understanding may be heard in the formula in the *Didache* 10:1.

this basic understanding that we can address the food and drink of the Lord's table: it will keep us going for this day, it is our daily provision, the rations for which we pray that the Father will give us daily. *Viaticum* is not the final eucharistic event but a basic eucharistic understanding. As such, it is an abuse of God's gift to countenance a restriction or refusal of this food to anyone who seeks it.

Appendix: A Focus on Food for the Journey

In this chapter I have argued that the shift in sacramental vision—which we can express in the shorthand: *viaticum* rather than "end"—is an important one for the Catholic Church and every other church, in itself and not just in terms of intercommunion. This shift is an inherent part of a development in the whole church's self-understanding of its liturgy that began in the nineteenth century and has been growing apace ever since. This shift is part of the project of renewing the very heart of our worship, so that it recovers from the detachment of which Cyrille Vogel wrote:

> Liturgy, which ought not to be anything other than the authentic expression of the community (lest it deny its very nature), has gradually been detached from the community throughout the centuries.[22]

It is reconnecting liturgy to the life of Christians, to their needs and witness within the creation, to their corporate life, and to their awareness of the closeness of God in the incarnate Word. But while the notion of this change in our way of viewing the eucharist is expressed in a lapidary phrase by Pope Francis, we should be aware of just how demanding this is. In this appendix I want simply to note two of the difficulties we encounter if it is to be more than another theological expression.

Food for a Journey

One of the challenges facing those who preside at liturgy is that once we begin to use a sacramental language that is rooted in our created experience we must reckon with the values of that language being perceived directly by those who use it.[23] We not only understand the notion of food, but we use it as an evaluating guide for our larger interpersonal experi-

22. Vogel 1972, 11.

23. This hermeneutical challenge extends across our liturgy; see O'Loughlin 2010a.

ence. If someone is describing a hotel and says "the food wasn't great," what is meant is usually more than a judgment simply of quality and cooking—it points to bad meal experience. If we describe the eucharist as "food for a journey," "sustenance for a pilgrimage," or "provisions for discipleship," then we have to attend to how that food—as in the actual sacramental sharing—is experienced.

This means that, at the very least, three topics must be examined:

1. In the world of Mass/Communion, the tabernacle was the place of the ciborium and that was the source of particles for the communicants. But the whole dynamic of the reformed liturgy is that it is the food over which we have offered thanks that is the food of the banquet. This means it is not sufficient to do this for some and then use a stored commodity, albeit a sacred commodity, for others, but it must be a clear message about our gathering. We have gathered to celebrate this banquet, to be thankful, and then to share this food as *our* food for *our* journey. Reservation is a sequel to our gathering—for the sick and for private devotion.

2. We speak of eating *and drinking*. Therefore, there must be an experiential correspondence between our talk and our actions. Likewise, if we are thinking of this gathering as being the source of our *viaticum* for our Christian lives individually and as a community, the drinking is as important as eating. So we must experience the natural combination of sharing "food and drink." This means that having the cup available at the eucharist for all must be the rule rather than the exception.

3. The language of the meal and sustenance is in most cultures, and explicitly in our culture because of its roots in Judaism, linked to the language of the table and having a place at table. The Lord prepares a table for us (Ps 23:5), we use table blessings, and we look forward to the time when "many will come from east and west and sit at table with Abraham, Isaac, and Jacob in the kingdom of heaven" (Matt 8:11), yet we do not provide an experience of being gathered around a table—at which we have been given a place by the Lord. For most Christians, most of the time, it is a case of an audience watching what happens at a table.

This need to match the experience to the language we use demands that authenticity rather than rubrical correctness becomes the watchword of our celebrating.[24] So, for example, we speak about breaking a loaf and we read Paul (1 Cor 10:17) on the significance of a single loaf, so we

24. O'Loughlin 2018a.

should actually have this so that words and actions form a single sacramental experience.

Food Is to Be Eaten rather than Looked Upon

We have, over the centuries, so detached the eucharist from the day-to-day life of the Christian struggle that we often fail to see how our theology of eucharist does not cohere with the spirituality of pilgrim discipleship we espouse. A very good example of this is our use of the word *altar*—where virtually all Catholics would simply see that as the descriptive term for an object in their local church building. Then having so named the object, they would define the word and so interpret the object in their building. But a glance at all the ancient altars that have survived from when Christians began to use this designation would show that what is found in our building is *not* like an altar but is actually a table. The confusion arose quite simply in the later second century when Christians who did not go to public altars, nor have private altars in the houses (and even the poorest house had at least one), were accused of atheism. The reply was to say that they had altars in the form of their tables. But very soon the word took a central place and it became a way of interpreting the eucharist, thus contributing in no small way to seeing the eucharistic action as an end in itself rather than an activity of Christians while on their journey. So we have to consider our ways of thinking and then ask if this is actually a vestige from a previous theological paradigm that has now but limited value. This is a problem affecting most churches, east and west, that places a high value on the eucharist.

One particular problem that affects Catholics—and from which the Orthodox and Reformation Churches are virtually free—is the cult of the reserved sacrament as a prominent aspect of devotion. With deep roots in the medieval period (especially the Corpus Christi procession), this cult took on a new dimension in the aftermath of the sixteenth-century Reformation with the rise of the adoration of the Blessed Sacrament, the movement of the vessel of reservation—the tabernacle—to become the very focus of most church buildings, and a range of spiritualities of the eucharist that had little role for actually consuming the elements. Thus the Blessed Sacrament became the sacrament of the end, life's goal present before one. This has become so embedded within Catholic practice that any attempt to change our understanding of the eucharist seems to wither once it confronts this inheritance. It is one of the great tasks that has yet to be addressed in many places. However, we need to continue to recall that the basic sacramental language is that of food and drink, and food is for eating rather than to be looked upon. It is in eating and drinking at table that we anticipate the banquet.

Food is often an object of admiration in human culture, we rejoice in the vision of a banquet laid before us, and we admire beautiful displays of food, but this is understood as anticipating the actual eating of the food. It is in eating food that it reaches its own finality—and this is equally true of our sacramental food. But we should not underestimate the difficulties (catechetical, practical, and emotional) facing us in making this shift toward a more incarnational model of liturgy.

8

A Theology of Divine Acceptance

There's no such thing as a free lunch!
—urban proverb

A very basic piece of the liturgical code, what we might call our ritual DNA as humans, is the way of contrasts: the world and the divine, matter and spirit, the profane and the sacred, this world and the other, reality and ritual, and on and on. Such oppositions are made almost absolute in the religious experience of many cultures, and variations on them often become defaults for Christians. But for monotheists this way of contrasts is deeply problematic. All is from God the creator: all depends for existence on God and there is no godless space in the universe. Not only does all depend on God, but there are the vestiges, the footprints, of God all through the creation. For Christians this is even more explicitly the case for we identify Jesus, whom we follow, with the Logos and confess that all things came to be through the Logos as there is a trace of the Logos in all that is. We can never dismiss the creation as just "stuff," nor can we imagine it as having within itself its own source of existence. It has its existence in him, the Logos, through whom it has come to be and is.

> In the beginning was the Logos, and the Logos was with God, and the Logos was God.
> He was in the beginning with God.

> All things came into being through him,
> and without him not one thing came into being.
> What has come into being in him was life,
> and the life was the light of all people. (John 1:1-4; my translation)

There is no thing that is outside the sphere of our relation with God, and at the very heart of our humanity is the place of encounter:

> And the Logos has become flesh and pitched his tabernacle among us, and we have seen his glory, the glory of the only Son of the Father. (John 1:14)

The tent (*tabernaculum*), the place of meeting of humanity with the creator, is among us; we encounter him not in an awesome otherworldly ritual but in a meal in what is a modified domestic space around a family table; and we encounter him in every righteous action that builds the kingdom of justice, love, and peace. But this leaves a nagging question: Is there no sense in which the liturgy stands apart from the everyday world around us?

For Christians the liturgy does stand apart from the everyday insofar as it models for us our future, but this is not solely the foretaste of the life of glory to come given to us now,[1] but it images for us the nature of what we are called to become here as the kingdom present among humanity. The liturgy should hint at the kind of world we Christians believe we should be building. In terms of the eucharist, it is the meal that should be: the kingdom modeled for us in this meal as the pattern for every meal, the values we see there as a vignette of the coming kingdom for which we pray. The otherness of our liturgy is not the vaguely sacral but a set of relationships that show what we are capable of with God's grace.

This kingdom-focused otherness is no simple matter. It was the failure of the eucharistic gatherings in Corinth to have at the core those precise kingdom-values (as distinct from the stratified values of a Gentile symposium) that provoked Paul's criticisms. Here the rich and the poor were not to be set apart—here the people were to wait upon one another, to

1. All Christian liturgy is anticipatory of the future, but it is also a celebration of God's love now; this was captured in the ambivalence of the phrase *pignus futurae gloriae* in the great antiphon *O sacrum comvivium*. *Pignus* is both a taste now and a pledge for the future.

serve each other rather than to grasp for themselves. Paul had a very clear sense that the values of the liturgical gathering were at odds with the values of the surrounding society, and when assembled the followers of Jesus had to live in the new way that flowed from being made part of the people of God.[2] Paul's aim is to contrast the liturgy that *should be* with the one that is there, the kingdom to come with the society round about it. Later, in the letter to the Romans, Paul made similar points about how the sharing of the food at their gatherings had to reflect who they were as Christians,[3] and in the letter of James there are other criticisms of how what is fairly standard party behavior, then as now, is not appropriate to their meeting.[4] Liturgy takes place in the world, in contact with the creation, but our manners and behavior must model the higher standard of the kingdom. Otherness is not a matter of ontological grade—only the Holy One stands apart from the creation and the divine nature is ineffable—that is somehow breached by ritual. The otherness of liturgy is that it should model a world free from sin that allows us to glimpse our future and that supports us as we "press on toward the goal for the prize of the heavenly call of God in Christ Jesus" (Phil 3:14).

But as those early documents witness to the failure to meet the standard of Christian liturgy in several first-century churches, so too our liturgy often fails this test. In 2005 I was in Seville Cathedral for Holy Thursday, and what struck me most forcibly was not that this was the beginning of the Easter Triduum but the hierarchy of church and state. There were the ranks of clergy each deferring to each other from "ordinary" parish clergy (not even in the entrance procession) to monsignori to the canons to the auxiliary bishops up to the cardinal—if these were all brothers, there was no doubt who was the eldest. Then there were the hierarchies of the state: of the city, of the province, and the representatives of the crown—each with a special place that dovetailed with the clerical hierarchy. Then there were the others, the baptized, who knew that they were "just there." I saw bowing (differing degrees) and genuflections aplenty—and that was apart from those prescribed in the rubrics. This liturgy modeled in its relationships the kingdom around it, but it did not even hint at the alternative values of the heavenly kingdom. It was a liturgy

2. 1 Cor 10–11.

3. Rom 14:1-6; see Jewett 2007, 846–47.

4. See Smit 2011.

that was deeply involved in ritual's role as social glue but with no visible concern with prophetic witness.

But sometimes, in the strangest places, we realize that the values of the assembly are at odds with those of everyday life. A famous First World War chaplain, the Reverend "Tubby" Clayton, defended the practice of his soldiers' club where over the entrance he had placed the sign "All rank abandon ye who enter here" with this account:

> I remember . . . one afternoon on which the tea-party . . . comprised a General, a staff captain, a second lieutenant, and a Canadian private. After all, why not? They had all knelt together that morning in the Presence. "Not here, lad, not here." [So] whispered a great G[eneral] O[fficer] C[ommanding] at Aldershot to a man who stood to let him go first to the Communion rails; and to lose that spirit [of equality] would not have helped to win the war, but would have made it less worth winning.[5]

For Clayton a key quality of liturgy—and he was thinking explicitly of eucharistic liturgy—is that it has a different set of values and embodies a different set of relationships to those of everyday. Moreover, those values (which they accepted when they knelt at the eucharist in that building in the morning) set a standard that they as Christians should seek to embody when they met in the afternoon. The liturgy is other in the sense that the deference at the heart of that military society did not belong there: "Not here, lad, not here."

This kingdom-modeling aspect of Christian liturgy establishes the need to distance ourselves from some of the attitudes of the wider society—such as those Paul heard about in Corinth—and that we positively adopt others, such as mutual service (Matt 20:26-27), that anticipate the reign of God. How does the question of intercommunion relate to this dimension of liturgy? This is a theme we can only explore by asking how our images of the kingdom can take on practical expression in what we choose to do and not to do in our liturgy.

5. Clayton 1919, 38. The officer in question was probably Field Marshal Sir Douglas Haig, who was the commander in chief of the British Army on the western front at the time the party recalled by Clayton took place; no greater difference in status could be imagined in the context.

The Merciful Welcome

As a community scattered over the continents and ages, we are held together by our shared memories, and without these even the most elaborate structures will be just so much transient bureaucracy. This common memory we perform and reperform, and at its core are stories from the gospels. In these stories the theme of the merciful welcome appears constantly. The memory of what we think of as "the church" may be full of negative images, powerbroking, and abuse, but what balances it is this image of the Father's love that we link to Jesus. These are images such as the story of the joy and banquet of the poor woman who found her coin (Luke 15:8-10), of the shepherd who rejoices over the found sheep (Matt 18:12-14), of the father of the prodigal son who throws his arms around the returned son and then throws a banquet for him (Luke 15:11-24). It includes tales of welcome and reconciliation such as Jesus eating with prostitutes (Luke 15:2), with outcasts such as Zacchaeus (Luke 19:1-10), healing a withered hand despite liturgical law (Matt 12:10-12), and taking a drink from an outcast Samaritan woman (John 4:7-42). Old divisions are not acknowledged in his welcome. Then there are stories of forgiveness like the story of the woman caught in the act of adultery (John 7:53–8:11) where forgiveness is so unconditional, and history simply canceled out, that they have seemed too potent to read at the liturgy lest they upset public order.[6] And there are other powerful images that speak of the unbounded love that comes from God such as that in Isaiah: "Let everyone who thirsts, come to the waters; and he who has no money, come, buy and eat! Come, buy wine and milk without money and without price" (55:1). And that at the Father's table there will be places for the outsiders: "I tell you, many will come from east and west and sit at table with Abraham, Isaac, and Jacob in the kingdom of heaven" (Matt 8:11).

These are not just "nice bits" encouraging a soppy imitation; rather, these are the very stories that constitute the proclamation of the kingdom. This vision, this kerugma, constitutes the real nature of what sets us apart, and they create an awareness within Christian consciousness that, while

6. Augustine, for example, believed that this story would lead to moral outrage—wives would find in it a justification of not being faithful to their husbands, and so he believed it should not be read in public (O'Loughlin 2000). Indeed, it was virtually never used in lectionaries.

God is beyond words and description, we can somehow appreciate the loving face that is turned toward us. Therefore, since we have to say something to ourselves of what God is, what we actually say is something to the effect that there is no limit upon God's loving welcome of us sinners. Unlike our immediately experienced world, the divine welcoming acceptance is without bounds—or, we just tell a story such as the parable of the Prodigal Son (Luke 15:11-24).

This then makes a demand on the liturgy to replicate that memory and hold this value—explicitly at odds with most of our human interactions—as a characteristic of our liturgical interactions. Any celebration at a table that claims to be the Lord's table, therefore, must promote a positive welcome to each and every person at the gathering. Conversely, any action that speaks of a lack of welcome and reconciliation fails to manifest this kerygmatic vision. And insofar as that human ritual fails to embody this kingdom vision, this otherness, it fails as "sacred liturgy."

A Liturgical Hermeneutic

But to say that a eucharistic celebration excluding a non-Catholic from full sharing on the basis that it seems unlike the father's reaction in a parable by Jesus seems trite. It could appear to be little more than the lampooned fundamentalism of those who invoke "What would Jesus do?" as a key to action. Such simple one-to-one correspondences not only fail to take account of our different situations, but they reduce the place of the gospel within discipleship to a collection of morality tales. Moreover, it assumes that exegesis is a matter of decoding a set of allegories. On such a reading we might just as well argue that it is the action of the son in returning to the father's fold that elicits the forgiveness, or argue that it is only the non-Catholic on "returning" to the church that could elicit welcome and, meanwhile, they should accept the famine as a consequence for having strayed! Such reasoning reduced God's covenant to just the sort of contract that belongs to everyday experience and is the very opposite of what values should exist in the liturgy. We do not decode our memories using formulae such as WWJD? but rejoice in them as revelations of the nature of our God.

The basis for the argument of the appropriateness of liturgical praxis mirroring our salient memory of the gospel lies in the way both liturgy and story speak about God. We might characterize the liturgy as a very special case of the way of analogy in the manner it recalls the nature of God to our minds and speaks to us.[7] But while this is theologically exact it is also inadequate. The liturgy functions as a poetic analogy: the words, gestures, events, the very food and drink of our eucharists are known in one sense but are also wholly open pointers to the infinity of God's love expressed toward us in the Christ. I cannot even seek to define the liturgy's meaning anymore than I could quantify God's mercy. The liturgy is a poem ever open to new discoveries of meaning and in this it resembles its Object. We can thus describe the liturgy as a *mysterium* because it creates an open space between us and the *Mysterium*. Then entry into the liturgy is neither theurgy nor a case of administering a duty that is owed by a creature to its Source, but it is to take part in myth. We use finite realities in a symbolic way because they can be transparent of transfinite reality. It is our meal, it is a human meal, but it is also the banquet of the kingdom.

The world of the parables as found in the gospels—and those stories about Jesus that function within those texts in the same way as parables, illuminating the nature of the kingdom—is also such a poetic world. A parable is not a Jesus-version of a fable by Aesop, but it is a glimpse into a mythic world where we can see what cannot be seen and experience what is beyond experience. A fable by Aesop contains a nugget of wisdom that is potentially accessible to any human being, but a parable or a miracle story or a tale like that of the visit of Jesus to the home of Simon the leper in Bethany (Mark 14:3 and parallels) only become meaningful within the community of faith among whom this is but a fragment of the whole reality of which they themselves are a part.

These two encounters with the Christian myth, liturgy and memory, cannot really be separated and both carry the community forward in its awareness of the presence of God. The mythic nature of both in imagining the kingdom make them indistinguishable in actual practice from our kerugma: we become what we preach, and we preach what we see ourselves as called to be. Both our gospel memory and our liturgical performance are dynamic within our imaginations. Both leave the world of finite understandings and fixed measures expecting us to engage with them in the way we engage poetically where it is the undefined that is our true object.

7. Let us think in terms of the classic exposition of analogy in the Western tradition in Aquinas's *Summa theologiae* I, q. 13.

This link between the liturgical myth of our rituals and the remembered myth of our story is still more complex in that both relate us to the divine in similar ways: we do not "get" a description of God's nature—much as we might desire this—but a genuine sense of God relating to us and the kind of relationship we need if we are to appreciate the mystery that is being opened up to us. Thus, for example, we hear of forgiveness from God, we hear of the need to practice forgiveness (Matt 18:22, for example), we seek forgiveness ritually, and we know that we must exhibit forgiveness. Moreover, if any part of this performance of the myth of salvation is omitted in story or ritual, then the whole becomes untenable; and we subsequently scramble to seek true propositions in the pieces. Indeed, when a lack of harmony is discovered between the memory and the current liturgy, then this dissonance serves to undermine the actual credibility of our proclamation.

In effect, this means that we cannot proclaim a vision of the messianic banquet and then not perform an anticipation of that banquet next Sunday. In the proclamation the human realities that convey the mystery are series of images expressed in words and sounds; in the performance those human realities are a gathering of people, a common table, a loaf, a cup of wine, and words and sounds and images—but both are rituals that anticipate an "other" that is not yet, but toward which we are invited in the Christ.

Places at the Banquet

This eschaton-focused otherness must be embedded in a series of "rules of thumb" for our liturgical action lest we slip back into the "otherness" of this world—an otherworld dichotomy within the human religious consciousness—a slippage that seems to shadow Christian worship down the centuries. If liturgy is to manifest the infinity of divine acceptance of each of us, then we must manifest that acceptance at our table. We do not see ourselves as defending his table lest the unworthy should partake, but rather we present ourselves as extending our table in its welcome so that it images the divine table's welcome. Presented in this way, a rule excluding a non-Catholic from the table is not only inappropriate but the very antithesis of the final message we are trying, each of us, to grasp and make part of our lives now in liturgy. It is from within the nature of the liturgy itself that we must understand the source of the need to practice intercommunion among Christians.

In the world of everyday values there is a piece of wisdom that we all learn to live by: "There is no such thing as a free lunch." We may sigh that this is the product of bitter experience, but it also coheres with our ontological status as finite beings of limited resources. It also fits with our Christian confession that God alone is wholly generous and all that we have is the consequence of his gift. But in the liturgy we seek to model this other world, one of generosity and love, and never more so than in making the act of eucharist central to our response. Our liturgy does not add to the divine glory but makes us more conscious of being as his gift in our thankfulness. Our liturgy is a performance of this, and so it cannot set limits to those who are its beneficiaries; and, parallel to this, our kerugma could be expressed: There *is* a free lunch!

9

Gathered as an Easter People

The Lord . . . went to James and appeared to him. Now James had already made an oath that he would not eat bread from that hour when he drank from the Lord's cup until he should see him risen from among those who sleep. . . . The Lord said: Bring a table and a loaf. He took the loaf, and blessed [God], and broke [it] and gave [a portion] to James the Just, and said to him: "My brother, eat your bread, for the Son of Man is risen from among those who sleep."
—the Gospel according to the Hebrews[1]

Our memory links our past to our present, gives us an identity, and tells us where we are now. Memory is not simply a recording process or a retrieval function, but a dynamic process by which we identify salient moments that make sense of what we are doing today. Hence, there is always an interchange "then" and "now."[2] This has a bearing on everything that we hold dear as Christians, but has a special relevance to the liturgy that replicates itself over time, and an even more special significance for the eucharist in that it explicitly calls attention to itself as a memorial and presents itself to us as a response to "do this in memory

1. This word is merely inserted to correct the tendency to see Jesus as blessing the bread; "God" is used as it assumes less in this context than *Father* or *Lord*. For an examination of the significance of this passage for the early history of the eucharist, see O'Loughlin 2009.

2. The notion of "salient memory" was developed by Schwartz 1982.

of me."[3] This memory-memorial dimension of the eucharist has some significant, and usually unrecognized, implications for the issue of intercommunion, not least because it highlights some deficiencies in the notions of the presence of the Christ and the eucharist across the Western churches.

I want to begin by inviting you, the reader, to take part in a small thought experiment. Consider for a few moments the range of images—pictorial or verbal—that are linked with the eucharist. In the forefront come images of the Last Supper—that meal just before his death that Jesus ate with the disciples on the evening before he suffered. Ever since the so-called "institution narrative" became part of most eucharistic prayers, this has been the dominant image forming a background to what we do. This is the image that can be found across Christian art and a moment's thought can bring a string of Last Suppers to mind. And, much of the incidental imagery of loaves and cups, grain and grapes, is seen to flow directly from the Last Supper. A little further consideration would bring to mind images that interpret the eucharist as the Anointed One's sacrifice and so images of crucifixion and of Jesus who has given his life for his friends (John 15:13). We might argue about how the Last Supper, the death on the cross, and the eucharist are related to one another—and Western Christians have done so for over four hundred years—but that the death of Jesus on the cross is somehow central to the eucharist is not questioned. Hence in Catholic churches while there might be a mural of the Last Supper, there will always be a crucifix. In recent decades this has often been the source of controversy (from the highly rubrical question of whether it must be visible to the presider as he utters the words of consecration to issues over whether it should be realistic or whether Jesus may wear vestments, or whether it should show Jesus dying or dead or risen), but the core image is that of the scene on Calvary. That these are the appropriate images to call to mind is as it should be—these are the eucharistic images that are linked to our proclamation—see 1 Cor 11:23—from before the time of any of the documents that later formed the New Testament. However, the memory structure within which these images of the moment of the Last Supper and the moment of the crucifixion are called to mind is more problematic.

3. 1 Cor 11:24-25; Luke 22:19.

For much of our history—certainly in the Western churches—we have engaged in remembering as recalling and reenacting a historical sequence of events in a single continuous time running from the time of Jesus up to today. Indeed, so embedded is the manner of remembering, and so close is it to how we recall other historical events, that we are oblivious to it. This needs some exploration. Let us place a series of events in sequence along a line:

399 BCE	Socrates dies
55 BCE	Julius Caesar invades Britain
ca. 4 BCE	Jesus is born
ca. 26 CE	Jesus preaches
ca. 30 CE	Jesus enters Jerusalem in triumph
	Jesus holds the last supper
	Jesus dies
	Jesus rises
ca. 50 CE	Paul becomes a Christian
ca. 58 CE	Paul writes to Corinthians
	. . .
ca. 1950 CE	our local church was opened

We then think of recalling these events today: so we have Christmas and recall the birth; philosophy teachers always trot out 399 BCE as a date that should be in students' heads; we recall the Last Supper at Mass; we recall the crucifixion at Mass; we recall the resurrection on Easter Sunday; and we will recall the seventy-fifth anniversary of our church building in a few years' time. This seems very straightforward: each act of memory is a matter of consciousness directly linked to a specific past moment—and we might go as far as to say that we reenact or make present that past moment *now* through ritual. That this is how we recall the past when we assemble can be demonstrated visually and textually. Consider how frequently the space between the front legs of the eucharistic table (the altar) is decorated with a scene of the Last Supper—sending the signal that the image presents the *then* moment, which is still the *now* moment for those who believe, or that this *now* is a repetition of the *then* to those who treat it solely as a human phenomenon. It is not so long ago that that same space under the front of the altar seemed an ideal shape in which to present an image of the dead Jesus lying in the tomb. The message was that Jesus has died for us and we reenact his death in the Mass but, in the words of older catechisms, "in an unbloody (*incruoris*) manner." The movement was from the death to the memorial of the death. We can see it textually in the way that the gospels were read (at least since the time of Eusebius of Caesarea at the end of the third century) as four reports in sequence of a string of events that could be reconciled to one another and paralleled with other events in one sequential timeline.

Post-Easter Consciousness

In contrast to these powerful images, we recognize in reflection that this is *not* what we believe we have in either the gospels or the liturgy because both are born out of resurrection faith. The gospels came into being as the preaching of those who believed that Jesus had risen from the dead and was alive and present among them. Their central concern was that Jesus had risen "in accordance with the scriptures," and these stories about him are presented within the framework of this resurrection consciousness. Likewise, the liturgy of worship to the Father could take place in the Christ because the risen Christ was among them. They had been buried and risen in the Christ in baptism (Col 2:12), and it is for the presence of Jesus that they are thankful to the Father in the eucharist (*Didache* 9:3-4). That Jesus is the Christ (John 20:31) and that Christ is risen (2 Tim 2:8) are what separate the followers of Jesus from the rest of the people of God. It is this post-Easter mind-set and faith that generated all their remembering whether it is of Jesus' genealogy, his birth, his deeds and stories, or of the events surrounding his death. It is the awareness that they are celebrating their meal with the risen Jesus that is the basis for their remembering the story of him, of all his meals both before and after Easter, and of the meal—the Last Supper—that is part of the Easter story.

When we engage in formal exegesis we have taken this postresurrection focus as central for the best part of a century, and it is the underlying presupposition of approach to the historicity of the gospels that these are not reporters' narratives but narratives formed from within the perspective of faith in resurrection, and thus faith in Jesus' resurrection (1 Cor 15:13) and in his continuing risen presence in the church. Both our gospel and our liturgy are responses to our faith in one salient event in the past continuing in our present: "God raised [Jesus] on the third day and made him manifest" (Acts 10:40).

We Celebrate the Paschal Mystery

This centrality then affects our perspective on the eucharist. We celebrate Easter every Sunday when we gather, and we celebrate the resurrection every time we celebrate eucharist. Hence the term that came to prominence in Vatican II and in the reform of the liturgy: the paschal mystery. The liturgy is our sharing in the whole event of his life-giving passion and his risen glory among us as the one and unique priest of the new relationship. But faced with this embracing mystery it seems an awful lot simpler to teach and think about it as a chain of events each imagined on its own: supper, death, tomb, empty tomb, more meals, appearances, ascension. The notion of the paschal mystery belongs within the lecture hall rather than the pulpit, and the way we practice the liturgy suggests that it is one of those ideas, akin to *perichoresis* or the *operationes ad extra*, that can be sidelined once examinations have been passed. The simplest way to see this is to note the frequency with which Catholic presiders will say something like "Christ will become present among us," implying that the risen One is not present in the assembly.[4]

Our basic confession at our gathering is that the Christ is risen, and it is his presence among us that makes this gathering a divine liturgy. Here lies one of the direct implications of an Easter-centered faith for intercommunion. Much of the bitter argument of the sixteenth century, seen by many still to keep us apart, is that we thought of the Christ's priesthood and the priesthood of the presbyterate and the church as a priestly people as historically connected realities without recognizing that all priestly activity within the new covenant is but a way of thinking of the risen Lord among us drawing all humanity in his paschal mystery. All our theologies have got bits of the picture right, and all have to some extent got it wrong by failing to see the entirety of the church's worship as taking place in

4. That the presence of the Christ was not to be conceived solely in terms of the consecrated species was one of the themes in Vatican II (*Sacrosanctum concilium* 7) and it has been repeated in several documents since (e.g., the *General Instruction on the Roman Missal* 7), but it has not, by and large, entered the common discourse of Catholics. See Diederich 1978.

union with the risen Christ who never abandons his people. An Easter people is a sacerdotal people who now *stand*, risen with him, before the Father. It was with this postresurrection consciousness that Mark preached Jesus as saying: "and whenever you stand praying, forgive, if you have anything against anyone; so that your Father also who is in heaven may forgive you your trespasses" (11:25). We all need that forgiveness—if for nothing else we need forgiveness for slovenly theology—and receiving and imparting it makes it inconceivable that we would then refuse anyone standing with us to receive from the table at which we gather.

It is this constant presence of the risen Jesus within the church that is the presupposition of liturgy (Matt 18:20), and the sharing of the loaf and cup of the eucharistic banquet is one of the ways of encountering the risen Christ who is present in all the baptized. If we are an Easter people, we cannot think in terms of some who eat and some who do not: all are witnessing in their eating and drinking to their confession that he stands now among us and we rejoice in him (John 20:19, 26; 21:4). And standing now among us he offers us, individually and as a group, the reconciliation that is the fruit of the paschal mystery: "Peace be with you."[5] We repeat this Easter greeting at every eucharist at the sign of peace affirming that even on the dullest day our assembly is trying to witness to resurrection light. But that leaves a question: Can we wish each other this gift of peace and then say to another witness to the Risen One, but you shall not eat? It is the risen presence of the Christ, forming us into the sacrament of his glorious body (Phil 3:21), that is the basis of our eating and drinking, so an exclusion is tantamount to saying that the person excluded stands outside the risen Christ.

The Character of Resurrection Living

The story cited at the top of this chapter did not become part of the four gospels at the time they emerged as "the four" sometime in the second century, prior to their becoming the canonical four.[6] But like so many other extra-canonical early stories, most famously the *Pericope de adultera*,[7] they

5. John 20:19, 26; note that the greeting is in the plural: *eiréné humin* (peace be with *ye*).

6. See O'Loughlin 2009.

7. Now found at John 7:53–8:11.

were valued by subsequent generations as preserving glimpses into why they followed Jesus.[8] Here we have a miracle story—tables do not simply happen to be there along a roadside!—that links the presence of the risen Jesus in the church, with joy, and with the eucharist in a very explicit way. We could think about it as a parallel to the Emmaus story (Luke 24:13-35)—and it probably comes from around the same late first-century or early second-century period. In it a disciple is freed from his sadness and given the joy of eating and drinking with the Lord. The resurrection is the promise of freedom and joy, and our eucharistic gathering is intended in its joyfulness to reflect this to us. Old limits have been set aside, new and fresh possibilities opened, and the joy of the party, the abandonment of normal restrictions that is part and parcel of *communitas*, all witness to resurrection. So, can we then have a narrow restriction on who may and may not eat? Can we have rules that hurt one of those who profess "He is risen!" and can we cause dissention among the baptized who have been united into the New People by his rising? I leave these as questions because it is only in pondering the incongruity contained in these questions that we discover that the current widespread Catholic practice is a contradiction to what the very heart of our liturgy wishes to affirm.

The Ethics of Resurrection

The Christ has conquered sin and death; he has risen and is victorious over all the powers and principalities that seek to bind us. This is visibly at the heart of the liturgy at Eastertime, and we know that it has an ethical dimension to which we as disciples must adhere: Life has conquered Death. Christians must stand for life and for that which affirms life, and so be willing to confront anything that belongs to destruction and death. We know this in all our care for the sick, our standing with the poor, or attempts to proclaim liberty to captives and the acceptable year of the Lord (Luke 4:18-19). We fail, often miserably, but we must keep it before us as what we are called to become. But does the ethics of resurrection have a liturgical dimension?

That there is such a liturgical dimension is certainly the case in matters of oppression and human rights. We have come to see that our liturgy

8. See O'Loughlin 2000.

must not be a screen upon which we project human inequality (though it still happens), exclude others on the basis of any number of biases or bigotries (though it still happens), or use the liturgy for the promotion of games of power (though that too still happens). Despite our failings in practice, our official rhetoric now condemns liturgical behavior that is incompatible with our Christian vision. But what of further embedding divisiveness among Christians? And, likewise, we need to note that sectarianism is a constant human temptation and that one simple way to encourage religious emotion is to stir up the emotions of them and us, of distrust, and even of hatred. The sectarian trope takes many forms, but it relies on the same set of human emotions that are played upon by demagogues and populist leaders and often with parallel results. It is part of the reality of what we have traditionally called original sin that a leader—in either religion or politics—often finds it easier to get followers by playing on distrusts and suspicions of others than to appeal to love and unity. The corrupt preacher knows that "othering" brothers and sisters in baptism, because they are in another church, will often galvanize their own support and vision. It rarely happens in Catholic communities today, but it has happened in the past, and it is always there as a temptation.

While our exclusion of those who are not Catholics from the table, nor Catholic unwillingness to eat (when welcome) at the tables of other churches, is not in itself sectarian, the fact that it raises tensions between Christians plays into the hands of those for whom sectarianism is an easy way to get a sense of identity. The very possibility makes change in Catholic practice desirable. The ethics of the resurrection mean that we must ever be building bridges, extending the hand of friendship and welcome, and we must visibly reject any statement or action that could be perceived to endorse sectarianism or division. The risen Lord has shared his life with all of us, so all of us are guests at the party.

What Is Most Apt?

An obvious counter to what has been written in this chapter, or indeed this whole book, is that you cannot make a direct deduction of a particular path of action from such a basic theological reflection. Once could, therefore, celebrate both Easter and have explicit conditions that those who so celebrate must meet, if they are to have complete participation in the center and summit of the liturgy. As a matter of strict implication this is perfectly correct: the conclusion is not entailed in the premises. But liturgy does not exist or operate in such a strictly deductive environment. Liturgy is better thought of as a work of art, a poem, a drama, or, to use its own image, "a new song" (Ps 149:1).[9] The liturgy cannot, indeed, be viewed as a matter of strict logic for that would reduce it to being a transaction between finite realities. And such a deductive manner of thinking would itself entail a complete grasping, or comprehension, of God. Rather than such a bizarre approach to the divine, the liturgy's relationship is one between a Mystery in itself, God, and ourselves who are also mysterious (Do any of us know the depths of our own identities?)—and this relationship exists within the sphere of our limitations as creatures. In our relationship with God we need liturgy precisely because anything with a lesser role for imagination would simply not be fit for our purposes. The liturgy is about the divine; it allows a relationship, and the terms of that relationship are not there "for God's sake" but so that they can be somehow grasped by us. Thus the generosity of God, which surpasses understanding, is somehow seen in the generosity of a feast that we can grasp because we can "feel" generosity at a human feast. Both the Last Supper and the final banquet are so valuable in our relationship with God because they are comprehensible and because we can engage with them by a sort of bridging activity from what we know in our experience. In liturgy we find ourselves in a conversation, but one that is in our human language. The conversation could therefore be described as one of images, shadows, hints, and suggestions—and this, which can appear so puny, is what we mean when we say the liturgy is an analogical discourse or a sacramental encounter.

In response to this poetic nature of our knowledge and relationship with God many medieval theologians developed the notion of what is apt or appropriate as a manner advancing our discourse. We do not ask whether this statement is true for that supposes that we also know exactly what is false, but rather is this statement more apt, more appropriate to what we want to say about God? And on this approach we do not arrive with categorical certainty of deduction nor the clear-cut certainty of a

9. This image of "the new song" has been used down the centuries as the characteristic of the church's worship. It is found on six occasions in the psalms—hence its familiarity to those who recited the psalms as the Liturgy of the Hours—and taken up in Isa 42:10 and Rev 5:9; 14:3.

restrictive law, but we engage in a constant quest for an ever more apt expression of that which is inexpressible.

This dimension of our liturgical decision-making affects every chapter in this book, but it is examined here because this is never more relevant than when we speak of resurrection and Easter faith. This is the case because all we say regarding resurrection (literally: the "standing up again") has to be said, encountered through myth. Many Christians in a post-Enlightenment world cannot bear this thought, and the very mention of myth causes an allergic reaction of repeated assertion of the "really real" variety, but it is still the case that new life of Jesus, and the new life of us as an Easter people, is beyond the categories of measurable time and space, and so we use myth. The Easter Vigil is a real statement that the Christ is risen, but it falsifies all we say about the reign of God to imagine that resurrection takes place just west of the International Date Line before it does so at Greenwich—or if I do say such a thing, mixing the mythic and factual orders, then I must do so showing that what I am saying is within the mythic frame.

Therefore, when we engage in the activities of liturgy (for instance, in eating and drinking at the eucharist) we have to view these activities as drama, poetry in action, rather than simply acts of alimentation or hydration, and we must ask whether our poetry is apt to the mystery we are seeking to encounter. One answer, the current basis of the position of the Catholic and some other churches, is to say that what would be signified in that eating and drinking would contradict what we imagine the meal says about the final state of the church in, to use another set of mythic images, its union with the Christ. So the present discipline is based within a poetry about finalities, but is, for that matter, firmly located within a mythic framework. But is there a more apt, a more fitting mythic narrative with which we could work? This chapter has argued that the central joy of our faith is that which we express in Easter—the bounds of death are released, the sense of liberation from the prison is manifest, the joy of a new springtime is just felt like the joy of a spring morning. Now in that range of mythic, poetry, art—or of "analogical imagination"[10]—does a generous sharing with all who are present seem more apt, more attentive to the tune, than not? This is a call for good judgment more akin to select-

10. I borrow the phrase from Tracy 1981.

ing a beautiful poem than to determining "the better reading" in an exercise in textual criticism. It is more a call for a "good sense" of what will help all assembled here for this liturgy of resurrection to be ever more truly appreciative of the gift of resurrection than a forensic judgment as to whether the rubrics' demands have been met. We exist most truly within a myth, and that which we experience as an internal contradiction, a dissonance between word and deed, can shatter it. We, as liturgical leaders, have a duty of care lest "the dimly burning lamp" be quenched (Isa 42:3; Matt 12:20). This is probably the greatest burden of responsibility borne by those who lead the liturgy, and it is far more extensive and subtle in its demands than any perceived duty toward canonical regulation.[11]

The Meals of the Resurrection

When I was an undergraduate, a fellow student, an atheist missionary, told me that he could demonstrate "on internal evidence" that the resurrection was bunkum, and consequently the whole Christian "thing" was but a tissue of lies. Normally I just smiled and passed on, but this time I decided to see the nature of the internal evidence. He pointed out that if Jesus were risen from the dead—and not just resuscitated—he must be a spirit, but, pointing to Luke 24:41-43, there was a record of "the risen Jesus" eating a piece of cooked fish. How could a spirit do such a thing was the question I was to ask, and then jettison the whole story as nonsense. There was only one mythic element in this student's cosmos: the myth of absolute comprehensibility.

The effect of the encounter on me was quite the opposite from that intended—and so I am thankful to him. I suddenly began to understand the significance of some of the authors, names like Rudolf Bultmann, whom I had heard referenced in class, and I glimpsed that liturgy was a great poem of human-divine dialogue where story reached beyond imagination. Liturgy was our new song, not a treatise compiling propositions.

11. This raises the larger question of whether liturgical responsibility is *vectoral*—a one-way responsibility toward the authority from which the liturgy as a given is imagined to come—or *relational*—a responsibility to those on their journey who are now taking part in *their* liturgy. This is not a matter of obedience versus disorder, but one of which good makes the higher demand of obedience. This is too large a question to examine here, but one that we cannot ignore; see O'Loughlin 2013a.

That question about Luke's story of the risen Jesus eating a piece of fish shone a spotlight on the fact that the early proclamation took place in the meal gatherings of followers. Whether it was fish or bread, whether breakfast or supper or simply "at table," whether it was Luke or the redactors of John and Mark or the author of the *Gospel According to the Hebrews* or in some other resurrection story,[12] these audiences experienced the presence of the risen Jesus in eating together. Can we really say "Jesus is Risen, Alleluia" and then say "Only those . . . can come to the table"? Our coming from east and west and north and south to eat together in the presence of the risen Jesus is truly a foretaste of new life.

12. Mark 16:14; Luke 24:35, 41-43; and John 21:9-15.

10

The Phenomenon of Conflicting Theologies

*If anyone says that in the most holy sacrament of the Eucharist the substance of bread and wine remains together with the body and blood of our Lord Jesus Christ and denies that wonderful and unique change of the whole substance of the bread into his body and of the whole substance of the wine into his blood while only the species of bread and wine remain, a change which the Catholic Church fittingly calls (*aptissime appellat*) transubstantiation, let him be anathema.*
—The Council of Trent, 1551[1]

One problem appears on the horizon the moment any mention is made, in a Catholic context, of intercommunion: non-Catholics do not believe in the Catholic theology or some particular aspect of Catholic theology of the eucharist. Moreover, there is a widespread belief that there is a single, virtually monolithic, and very consistent teaching on the eucharist.[2] Having been expounded in literally hundreds of magisterial pronouncements, it is now a matter upon which the Catholic Church has a

1. Session 13, On the Sacrament of the Eucharist, canon 2 [= Denzinger 1652] (Fastiggi and Englund Nash 2012, 397).

2. This belief can be seen in the 1983 *Code of Canon Law* when it states that a pastor is "to explain the doctrine" of the Eucharist with the greatest care (Canon 898).

well-known position, and so anyone who stands apart from this position must be somehow repudiating that teaching.

This process began at the time of the Reformation, and the various decrees from 1520 to the close of the Council of Trent made it explicit that anyone who subscribed to what Catholic authorities took to be the positions of the Reformers was excommunicated for taking that position. Since then some subtle changes have taken place in Catholic attitudes. First, the attitude to the condemned propositions has subtly shifted in focus: now these are the positions of others and they can be seen as in an either/or relationship to Catholic theology. Whether or not the actual positions condemned at Trent actually represent any theologian's position in the sixteenth century or any individual or group of Christians today is not what is relevant here, but rather the sense that there are two bodies of doctrine, *ours* and *theirs*, which somehow contradict one another, so that if someone is not fully with us, then there is an implicit denial of what we are saying about the eucharist. If that were the case, we would find ourselves letting the sacrament be insulted if we let someone receive it on his or her own terms. They must receive it on the church's terms (church here being identical with the *catholica*) or be barred. Second, that somehow accepting this "very clearly set-out doctrine" and belonging to the [Catholic] Church are identical realities; to the extent that not accepting this doctrine—expressed as "believing it"—is the same as willfully choosing to wish to reject the church. In this case, anyone who will not sign up to the doctrine does not want to be part of the church—and so saying that that person is allowed to receive communion is to engage in a meaningless activity—and so respect for the sacraments means they should be barred.

This thinking is, of course, neither the formal teaching, nor the precise way to interpret canonical documents, nor does it take account of all the nuances that are inherent in doctrine, but it is widespread. And, as the operative theology—what is accepted by clergy in their praxis, its influence has been widely pervasive. It is this general approach, for instance, that underlies so many of the exceptional cases that are found in official guides to when a Catholic minister could, on a case-by-case basis, admit a non-Catholic. Equally, it is observed that it would not affect intercommunion with the Orthodox churches—as they are not expected to adopt Catholic theology—but this does not really emerge as a problem in pastoral practice. Rather this attitude to the link between adopting a particular theology and ecclesial belonging is something that belongs among the Western churches and it can hardly be separated from our memory of four hundred and fifty years of Catholic-Protestant strife. In effect, it means that the eucharist has a become a lightning rod for identity: to be a Catholic is *to believe* in a particular set of theological propositions, and this doctrine is like an ideology that defines the group. If you do not *believe in* this particular theology, then you are outside the church.

This blending of faith, belonging, and a specific theology can even be heard in the words that Pope Francis used in his reply to Anke de Bernardinis. He said: "It's true that in a certain sense to share is to say that there are no differences between us, that we have the same *doctrine*." The supposition of this is that it is sharing the same doctrine that makes eucharistic sharing possible. But is this not putting a great deal of weight on the words of theologians down the centuries, and is it not tantamount to saying that we have the doctrine so well elaborated that this theological formulation is virtually equivalent to revelation itself? Can one ever be said *to believe in* a theology, in any case? I may hold it as my certain and fixed position—my "belief" in the epistemological sense—that a certain theological formulation is the best that can be arrived at, but this is not to be confused with my *faith*—belief as a religious act—which is in God, his goodness, his revelation of himself, his acts, and, most especially, his sending of his Son as the man Jesus.

Theology and Ideology

Since the beginnings of scholasticism, with the condemnation of Berengarius of Tours in 1079, the Western church has considered the eucharist as one area where theologians should work with verbal precision: one wrong use of a term could mean academic dismissal, ecclesiastical censure, and worse—as in the case of the execution of Jan Hus in 1415.[3] Already there had been a devotional revolution with regard to the eucharist by which the actual material used in the liturgy, a loaf of bread and a cup of wine, became the objects of the liturgy: these items became the sacrament and their being the sacrament was one end in itself of the liturgy, and so of the presbyterate. There was a general acknowledgement by theologians that this was not a complete treatment of the eucharist, but how it related to that larger picture (usually designated as the "the eucharist as sacrifice") was none too clear.

3. On Hus and the eucharist, and significance of the events surrounding Hus's life for ecumenical discussions today, see de Vooght, 1960.

However, this focus on the elements not only accorded well with a spirituality in which usually none but the celebrant (a single individual) spoke, and the elements were observed in awe rather than eaten and drunk by other Christians present. This focus on a change was also eminently suitable for the concerns of the canonists: any change was the result of a cause and that presupposed the possession of a power—and the use of powers was regulated by law. Similarly, a concentration on objects and changes in objects fitted well with a style of philosophical analysis that was used to describe and to arrange objects within the universe. So an object could be described in terms of substance and accidents, matter and form, and potency and act within a rather rigid set of "causes." It seemed reasonable that as this was excellent for explaining the material world around them, so it should be adaptable to the whole of creation. While few of the authors of such theological books imagined that it was as simple and clear-cut as that, all the subtle qualifications—such as that found in the canon quotes above where it does not say "this is transubstantiation" but merely uses this word as a label, and where it does not say this is the only word but simply "the most apt," and so a better word might come along—were lost in transmission. The general view was that everything was all wrapped up. Unfortunately, few of the fundamental issues in the debate were anything like as unproblematic as the general view held them to be.

The best example of this is the Latin word *substantia*, which was central to all the debates. Every young student was told it came from Aristotle, but he used the word in a great variety of ways, so it was anything but clear what it meant in even the simplest context. Indeed, it was not even certain which Greek words it was translating at any time. Was it the equivalent of *ousia* or *hypostasis* (both Greek words with already complex histories in Christian theology) or *hypokeimenon* or *entelecheia*, or some other word? It had yet other meanings derived from its use in Latin (it was a technical term for Boethius), and it had other meanings derived from the Arabic commentators. Moreover, once it was used in a metaphysical account its meaning changed depending on how that scholar constructed a vision of reality: one only has to recall the bitter disputes between the Thomists and the Scotists to know that *substantia* was problematic.[4] Moreover, once it was used with reference to the eucharist, it developed even more meanings such that an accident could be thought

4. The scholarship on this topic is vast, see, for example Macy 1984; 1992; 1994; and Adams 2010.

of having a separate existence from a substance—an idea unknown until theologians claimed they had just taken over a language from the logicians or the philosophers. This confusion can still be seen today when Catholics are most willing to affirm their belief in transubstantiation—and possibly willing to deny *consubstantiation* (which it is assumed is just as consistently believed by the Reformation churches)—but are unable to explain what they mean by "substance." The usual explanation is derived from a notion of substance used in chemistry, and quite unlike any meaning given to *substantia* prior to the time of Baruch Spinoza in the mid-seventeenth century. Moreover, any attempt to see which corresponding theory they wish to employ to explain the continuance of accidents without a substance usually means the invocation of the miraculous and, thereby, another call to faith. In significant contrast the notion that the theological inheritance is clear and precise, the medieval legacy that was so controversial for the Reformers and that was apparently codified by Trent, is massively confused, imprecise, and ill-adapted to any larger theology of the eucharist.

It is, therefore, even more regrettable that as the communities pulled apart in the sixteenth century, and their eucharistic gatherings were the most obvious expressions of this divide, that for many Catholics the separation was perceived as a departure due to nonacceptance of the "Catholic teaching" about eucharistic change and the sacred presence within the elements. The result was that for Catholics it was a clear choice between accepting this theology, as they perceived it, or Protestantism—and this theology now took on the characteristics of the kernel of Catholic ideology, and a particular set of practices that were seen to reflect this became the cultural markers of belonging to the Catholic Church.

At this stage we could note three interim conclusions. First, we have an inherited tendency to think of certain parts of our theological inheritance as forming a coherent eucharistic doctrine that is well nigh set in stone and virtually equivalent to the revelation of God. Clearing up such confusions is a good thing in itself—it has been at the core of the whole liturgical reform—but it has special significance for how we relate to other Christians around the table. If such "Catholic doctrine" has become a marker of identity, then one position in a theological debate has become a group ideology, and if sharing that is the criterion of admission to the table, then we have reduced membership of the church to belonging to a religious party. We do not gather at the Lord's table because we are ideologically *pure* (the parallel is to having voting rights in an organization because you are a fully paid member in good standing). We are able to stand at the table because we have a relationship with Jesus the Christ through baptism—and our standing there is not a measure of our adherence to any particular doctrine, much less our willingness to be identified with a religious party, but because giving thanks to the Father is a basic need recognized in our discipleship, and because we need to be resourced from the Lord for the daily taking up of our cross in following him (Mark 8:34). If eucharistic participation is somehow dependent upon a particular ideological purity—"you have the right theology, so you can take part"—then we have subordinated the mystery to our own attempts to define it.

Second, the scholastic approach to theology has altered, possibly irrevocably, how the Western churches approach every question of faith and so we are eminently familiar with the methods without ever being formally trained in them: we can dig and dig, refine and refine, argue and argue. But if there are two areas where those methods, essentially the method of a lawyer prosecuting a case,[5] are limited, it is in relation to (a) liturgy understood as a real group event rather than simply a text for analysis, and (b) in appreciating the contexts and historicity of inherited texts whether they be canonical or not. Yet it is in these areas that some of the greatest modern achievements in theological understanding have taken place. We think of liturgy in a far more holistic way today than as a text (to be checked for consistency with other texts—that is, orthodoxy) legally performed (the demands of rubrics). Likewise, we know the dangers of reading a text, such as a gospel, as if it were a collection of logical propositions. These studies have shown to us that the eucharist is far larger than the issues discussed during the Reformation—and indeed that how we relate to liturgy is as important as the liturgy itself. From a Catholic perspective this is most clearly seen in our recognition that the eucharist is not the private action of a presbyter *for* the people of God, but the action of the whole community with a presbyter presiding. This is the big picture that underlies the reform and that, half a century after Vatican II, is still very much a work in progress. But it should remind us of something else besides: the reality of the eucharist is always greater than our attempts to tie it down in Cartesian-style "clear and distinct ideas." The aim of our theology is to help us explore ever more fully the mystery and through critical reflection to see if we are engaging in the

5. See Kuttner 1960.

activity of Christian thanksgiving to the best of our ability. Our model of eucharistic theology should not be the definitions and exclusions of Trent but Paul, who sought to expand the Corinthians' imaginations of what they were doing when they engaged in the eucharist and who, noting the defects in their ways of doing this, proposed a liturgical reform.

Third, there is a dangerous tendency in all religions to imagine that their understanding is now complete and that they are at the end of history: change, whether improvement or decadence, is now beyond them. This attitude certainly took hold of the Catholic approach to the eucharist after Trent: the doctrine was complete and the rubrics ensured continuity. But it was an illusion. We are always changing, and history is dynamic and open: so our religious response must always be that of seeking growth and correcting our limitations. Theology is neither a monolith nor complete. Doctrine is not a file to be downloaded, but a constant activity to say something that is meaningful about the divine love toward us, and to say this in as adequate and reverential a way possible. Likewise, just as our theology and understanding is always developing, so also is that of every other church. To imagine, for example, that another church today is an adherent of what we Catholics defined "consubstantiation" to be in the 1550s—and then make that the basis for practical action, such as excluding someone from the table—is simply absurd. All Christians struggle to understand what the Lord is calling us to do as his disciples, and just as theology among Catholics has changed massively so has the eucharistic understanding of other churches, and it continues to do so.[6] The best evidence of this is not documents like *BEM*—to an extent a deliberately backward-looking document seeking to bandage old wounds—but, rather, the fact that virtually every church has renewed its liturgy in the past fifty years and most place, just as Catholics do, a greater emphasis on understanding liturgy not simply as the performance of rites or the fulfilling of ordinances but the celebration of who we are in Christ.

Sources of Theology

Churches today, by and large, appreciate that they are not going to tie down what the eucharist means in a few sentences or in some confession of faith to be used as a kind of border guard. Equally, the desire to have

6. For an example of a very recent development in one church's evolution in thinking about the eucharist, see Wilson 2018.

a theological microscope, the desire to explain how and why something happens or does not happen (which was the great aim of so many theologians on all sides in the sixteenth century), is now a thing of the past. When we do find Christians engaged in such microscopy, we find that, sadly, they also believe that theology is a possession of one group, their ideology, and that their model of Christian interaction is one of conflict rather than dialogue. The opposite view that doctrine is a searching and something open, equivalent to what Pope Francis refers to as "a journey," seems all too fuzzy and incomplete. Moreover, should we not strive for a single doctrine of the eucharist and see if people and churches would not sign up to it? Would this help solve the problem of intercommunion? First, this is again a manifestation of the notion that a eucharistic theology is an ideology, and so participation at the table is a consequence of adherence to a particular theological position. Second, such a uniform theology is itself an illusion: it has never existed, and it cannot exist. Indeed, the uniformity that is assumed in Catholic practice (if you are baptized a Catholic, then you accept Catholic eucharistic doctrine and, therefore, can receive communion) is little more than a legal fiction to maintain the consistency of Catholic canon law.

So why is a single consistent doctrine an illusion? Let us imagine a Catholic parish community in a suburban setting today. It has about four hundred people at two gatherings over a weekend, one on Saturday evening and one on Sunday morning, and there is a larger Catholic population of 1600 people who vary from those who are culturally Catholic in that they seek our liturgy only for the rites of passage to those who make occasional visits to the community's assemblies. Being a suburban parish it has a good mix of ages, and there is a steady coming and going of people, some of whom have come to work there for a while before returning to their homelands. Some are there because they are students, and some have been born and bred there. Every variation on the human condition is there and the whole assembly is reminiscent of the diversity of humanity in Acts 2:1-12. In this gathering, how many understandings of the eucharist are present, and what does this variety say about the link between Catholic doctrine and Catholic celebration?

In any member of this community we could isolate three sources that contribute to what that person understands about what they are doing, the meaning they give to this, and the degree of attachment they have to that understanding (what we might call their *beliefs* about this activity).

First, there is the liturgy itself, and its content which, thanks to the renewal of the liturgy following Vatican II, now impacts directly on Catholics in a way it had not done for more than a millennium. For some, this is Mass, and so long as you are there, you are there, and you have taken part and there is little more to worry about. This is a time for one's own prayers and devotions, which are fitted in around standing, sitting, kneeling, and making certain well-known responses. For another, it is the words of the eucharistic prayers that hold the key. For someone else it is the sense of community that is the emotional key, and for that person's neighbor its meaning is in a verse of a hymn. Side by side there will be someone who wonders what all this rigmarole regarding the readings is about and would rather just get to "the main event" and someone who is not quite sure what a eucharistic prayer adds to readings and prayers. Most are agreed, however, on the fact that the sermon is too long and boring. Moreover, this variation is not simply the fact that each person makes sense of their own experience for themselves, but while in one place the Prayer of the Faithful is presented as an important element in the exercise of the priestly intercession of the priestly people, in another those prayers are a begging list trotted out as a formula.

Such an admission usually provokes an immediate reaction that the liturgical reforms of Vatican II simply ushered into the Catholic Church the monster of *tot homines, quot opiniones*, with people deciding for themselves what they think. Unfortunately, bidden or unbidden, the individual mind will make sense of what it sees and hears. In the days of a virtually silent Mass, which was further screened from perception in other ways, those attending still sought to make sense of what they could or could not see. So the actions were the subject of allegory, the bells portended the dangerous significance of the events, while the words were silent lest they be overheard by the unworthy or demons. The less that any action is transparent or statement pellucid, the greater the misconceptions they will generate in those who perceive them.

Even though all those people in our fictional parish are gathered at a single event, there are as many stories of what that event means as there are people in the gathering. However, in each the Holy Spirit is present, and offering that person the possibility of growing in the mystery of God.[7]

7. O'Loughlin 2016.

The second source is that which we most easily identify: teaching, catechesis, and instruction—surely here there is a single doctrine or, at least, there could be a single "party line." They will have heard explanations of the eucharist, stories about the eucharist, and umpteen introductions to why they have gathered. These will have been spread over a period of perhaps half a century and will have come from pastors or teachers of every stripe. Some will have worried and queried this time; and, again, another will just assume that it is all settled. One will repeat, if asked what they are doing, what was learned as a child preparing for First Communion; another will be an adult convert who learned about the eucharist during her journey through the Rite of the Christian Initiation of Adults and was baptized only last Easter. Some will have interpreted everything within a world of poetic imagination, though they may never have opened a novel; others will hear it all as positivists seeing the world as a collection of empirical facts, though they have never taken a course in philosophy. A homily may be given over to an exposition of the teaching of Trent but will interact, and produce a new theology, with a listener who is a member of a scripture study group; a different theology will be formed in the mind of a member of a group who works to alleviate poverty; and someone else just might be spending the time trying to locate the preacher's background somewhere on the Thomist spectrum.[8] Again, this might seem like a cacophony reminiscent of Babel, but recall that we can write books on how master and pupil, Ambrose and Augustine, could produce different theologies of the eucharist. Rather than the dystopic vision of Genesis 11, we should rejoice in the variety and richness of human understanding as a reflection of the creative exuberance of God, and pray for the Spirit's work that, each in his or her own voice, will tell of the mighty works of God (Acts 2:11).

But the diversity of understanding is even deeper because, before anyone arrived at that Sunday's liturgy or any formal liturgy, and apart from anything that someone heard or saw in a teaching situation, every sister and brother has picked up material from the culture forming their views of the eucharist. While an expert in popular beliefs could study this in detail,[9] I shall simply pick out three stories from my own experience. First, a butcher left a stipend to get a Mass said for his intentions, then he re-

8. See John 1966.

9. See Lysaght 1991.

turned and doubled the gift saying to the priest: "Put in a bit of extra umph, I need to get the ear of the Man Upstairs!" The intention was that he would win the contract to supply meat to a hospital. We might dismiss this as superstition, but every university chaplaincy sees a rise in the size of congregations around exam time, and Pope St. Gregory the Great taught a story of a fixed number of masses having a liberating effect for a soul in purgatory—and "Gregorian Masses" and "Month's Minds" are still part of many Catholic cultures.[10] Second, a little child was causing mayhem in a shop, and the exasperated mother shouted: "If you don't stop right now, you won't be making your First Communion. Only good kids can go to Holy Communion." All the hours of catechesis in the school and the parish might not have sunk in as deeply as that threat, with the result that another Christian has made a nearly indelible connection between the eucharistic feast and the rewards due to good behavior. Third, a group of Spanish religious sisters who had founded a new house for their order were finding their first winter in a draughty house almost unbearable. After all, they were living in Britain but wearing habits designed for Andalucia! One of their first actions was to knit a thick woolen jumper to be placed over the silk veil over the ciborium in the tabernacle: "Poor Jesus," explained one nun: "It is terrible he has to live in this cold house." We might suggest that they had confused the physical and sacramental orders of existence, but then we might read the profession of faith prescribed for Berengarius in 1059 and think again.[11] The human mind is never a blank canvas; the intellectual *tabula rasa* is a dream of those who imagine that education is analogous to filling a pitcher. Rather, we should reread Augustine's *De magistro*, which insists that God is the only teacher and what we do, rather, is seek to deepen our own understanding and, then, nudge our brothers and sisters toward the truth.

Rather than engaging in a game of legal fictions that our assembly is made up of two clear categories—(a) a large group (labeled Catholic) with one orthodox and sufficient doctrine of the eucharist present at our assembly and (b) a few people (labeled non-Catholic) who have a different doctrine—we should face reality honestly. There are many understandings present every time we celebrate—some good and life-affirming, some askew and life-denying, and some just daft—and declare that having

10. See O'Loughlin 2009a.

11. Fastiggi and Englund Nash 2012, 234; and see Chadwick 1989.

a better appreciation of the mystery is a work in progress. If we see having a better theology of the eucharist as part of the pilgrimage of the church, rather than excluding non-Catholics we should welcome them fully as bringing yet other perspectives to the gathering. Indeed, these understandings may be new, different, and challenging.

Many Theologies, One Activity

For many people the notion that there is not a single, defined Catholic doctrine of the eucharist is, itself, a cause of surprise, because for centuries the Catholic Church has imagined that this was the case, and there is still an echo of that position in canon law. Moreover, other Christians who wanted to define their position in opposition to Catholicism were equally clear that there was a Catholic position that could be refuted—and if one took Trent at its word, and thereby assumed that it was the Catholic doctrine, then one indeed had a text with which to engage.[12] But having a legally agreed upon text is not the same as saying that this statement equates with the liturgy. This leads us to another, much larger, question: How do we envisage the relationship of doctrine and liturgy?

Since the beginning of scholasticism there has been a pecking order within theology that placed doctrine—whether one called that simply *theology* or *dogmatics* or, more recently, *systematics*—at the top. This was the real core of what we believe and other concerns, now compartmentalized as "disciplines," took subsequent places. This might be challenged by the exegesis of scripture, but usually the systematicians won and scripture was presented as a source of theology. Then there were the matters that flowed from theology, and first among these was moral theology (sometimes with its derivative status clearly labeled by being called *applied theology*), then there were even further derivatives such as *ascetical theology*—and more recently *spirituality* and the *de facto* regulation of

12. Few Protestant Christians have shared the training in scholastic categories that allows them to enter this language game and exploit its inherent contradictions, but one who did was the nineteenth-century Anglican theologian Richard Whately (1857, 78–91, where he discusses "intention"). What sets Whately apart from more recent theologians is that in his book we meet a case of religious *antagonists*; his approach could hardly be described as eirenic: both he and his opponents believe they can have a complete and comprehensive doctrine of the eucharist.

religion in the study of canon law. There were also the really poor relations grouped together as *pastoralia* and interesting sidelines such as church history. Out there on the fringe was *liturgical studies*, which was, at best, seen as working out doctrine in a ritual way and, at least, making sure that the rubrics were kept to a minimum standard. Changing this perception has been a topic of every Vatican document on theological education since *Mediator Dei* (1947), but the inherent culture of the classroom means that it is far from past. We think of faith in terms of theological content and intellectual decision, and, therefore, we imagine that there is a preexisting doctrine of the eucharist that is then expressed in a sense-perceptible form in the liturgy. We start with a body of doctrine, and we think of this as having been manifested in ritual.

There are two statements that are seemingly so similar that we often find it hard to distinguish them. The first is that a ritual act, such as the eucharist, embodies a theology, and the second is that a theology of the eucharist is embodied in every ritual act. Once we can see that these are *not* equivalent, then we can go some way down the road to reconciling some of the quarrels that have arisen between Christians. The first statement describes the situation of two or more human beings engaging in an activity because this is part of their behavior as who they are. Then, reflecting on that action we can discover how what they have done and said tells us about their understanding of themselves, human nature, the cosmos, and ultimate reality. On the basis of what we have discovered in reflection, we can then appraise whether such activity is good or bad, and whether it is consistent with their other activities, their publicly declared statements, and what some of the participants in the activity have said elsewhere. Here the content of the reflection—which we could organize academically—is a derivative of the activity, but then it is used to help appreciate the *significance* of what they are doing and perhaps change what they are doing in light of the reflection.

In the second statement, one begins with a body of ideas expressed as statements that are held to be true. These statements may take the form of a corpus of ideas (such as the Bible, the Nicene Creed, or the decrees of the Council of Trent), which then are studied and assembled into an intellectual edifice. This may be highly structured and can, and often is, studied as just such an edifice. Then one asks how this edifice is expressed in the practical life of the church or the lives of individual Christians. Thus, on the basis of a systematic body of knowledge, doctrine, one can determine what should be the attitudes of Christians to certain social phenomena, or whether there is a Christian moral position on certain actions. One can then ask how this body can be given shape in the actions of worship. Here we can say that doctrine underpins worship, whereas in the first statement we can say we have uncovered a theology *implicit in* worship.

The Western churches have tended to adopt the second approach and see liturgy almost as an analogue to the "learn-through-play" approach to teaching children. In this scenario we soon start asking questions such as "Is the liturgy a symbol?" or "Is it just a sign?" because we are troubled about how it relates back to the more profound, primary reality of doctrine. But a human action is a human action—so long as it has not been eviscerated of content through being made a token affair—and it does not have to be a manifestation of something other than itself.

Our starting point is that the people of God engaged in an activity at the beginning of every meal, thanking God for providing the food, and then again at the end thanking God for the enjoyment that comes from eating and sharing a meal. This action, rooted deep in the human awareness of dependence, was what was called for by who they were—and so it was codified in their perception of themselves in the law (Deut 8:10), and this recurrent action was explained and its significance spoken and written about.[13] This discourse was their doctrine, but this was a spinoff of an action. Jesus engaged in this action, changed the action, and handed on the action to his followers, and he may have drawn out from that action the significance of what they were doing. They engaged in the action and then spun out a variety of significances such as we see in Paul, the *Didache*, and the gospels. Paul studied the activity in Corinth and then drew out the significance of what they were actually doing, compared it with their vision of who they were as disciples, and then instructed them to do it properly. Paul reformed not their doctrine but their practice. The core of the *paradosis* is the bodily memory of *what we do together*, not what we declare to be what we deem to be the best explication of what we do (doctrine). It is always worth recalling that the words we so venerate liturgically from the gospels regarding the eucharist are a command, in the plural, to do something: *touto poieite* (Luke 22:19); and it is followed

13. See LaPorte 1983; and Bokser 1984.

by a second command to action: *phagete* (Matt 26:26).[14] It is not a command to *believe this* or *have this* or *hold this* or *look upon this*. It is sobering to notice that Paul does not see the proclamation of the mystery of faith as a matter of words, as often in the contemporary Catholic liturgy, but in the activity of eating and drinking together: "For as often as you eat this bread and drink the cup, you proclaim the Lord's death until he comes" (1 Cor 11:26).

On this count, it is the eating and drinking together, rather than the doctrine to which any of the participants subscribe, that constitutes the reality of the mystery. This experience can then be examined for its meaning for the individuals and the group, and its implicit theology explored. Therefore, assuming that someone is willing to eat and drink at a Catholic celebration of the eucharist, is there any basis for excluding them because of a difference in doctrine?

We should now observe a corollary of this question were it to be answered in the affirmative—as it implicitly is answered in current Catholic common practice—and hold that differences in doctrine do constitute a barrier at the table. This position actually generates an absurdity, because if common and correct doctrine is that important as a presupposition to action, then we should examine each participant on each occasion to ensure a sufficiency of knowledge and orthodoxy (quite apart from moral rectitude). Thankfully, common sense has normally intervened, and we do not quiz people on the finer points of doctrine or check whether clergy have such a learned understanding of *substantia* that they could affirm an acceptance of transubstantiation. Consequently, to raise a question about doctrine regarding a member of one of the churches of the Reformation (we would never think of it with regard to an Orthodox Christian whether or not they would use our categories) is simply a discriminatory anachronism.

Moving Forward

That we should address how we view the relationship of our eucharistic activity to our doctrine is hinted at in a few brief words of Pope Francis to Anke de Bernardinis:

14. These references are not intended as a historical reconstruction of some sort of primitive "institution narrative" but merely to note how the commands to perform actions are part of our liturgical memory; see O'Loughlin 2014.

> But a friend who was a Pastor said to me: "We believe that the Lord is present there. He is present. You believe that the Lord is present. And what is the difference?" Alas, they are explanations, interpretations. Life is greater than explanations and interpretations.

By placing life—the actions and events together that go to making up our life—before the formulations of belief, the pope is prioritizing what is actually happening. Moreover, in seeing what may be differences in doctrine as *explanations* and *interpretations*, he is demoting doctrine to what the scholastics would have called "the order of second intentions." All Christians should heed the call to act: to gather, to thank, to eat, and to drink. Only when we have all done that, and done it in a humanly adequate way as distinct from engagement with tokens, should we turn to concern ourselves with having ever-better explanations.

11

Where Do We Need to Go from Here?

The liturgy is and remains the centre of the life of the church. If this can be successfully renewed, won't that also have effects on all the areas of church activity?
—Hans Küng[1]

In the course of writing any book, even a short book like this one, a dark thought seems to sneak into my mind and ask whether it is really worth the labor, whether it is not all a tiresome waste of time, and whether there are not better things that I could do with my time. After dismissing it as just a natural doubt such as one gets in the course of any task, the doubt returns and starts listing all the reasons the book is not worth the paper. In the case of the present book, first, it is a technical problem, and sensible people will not get caught up in these arcane problems; they will just practice intercommunion. Second, those who do worry about them, such as older clergy so concerned with regulations, that even if they read this book and agreed with it, they still would not alter their practice. Third, many younger Catholic clergy belong to "the new right" and are into identity theology, and hard demarcations give them a sense of belonging and self-confidence. Fourth, bishops will not change because many think that the "Francis phenomenon" will pass, and so they wait for top-down

1. Küng 2002, 285.

change. And, fifth, faced with major problems both outside the church-sphere (such as climate change and issues around population growth and food security) and inside it (such as safeguarding and taking action on abuse by clergy, or the need to reinvent ministry in the Catholic Church, or the need to find a new language for the proclamation in a secular age), this is a dispute with many words but with little at stake. At that point I switched off my computer and went for a long walk, declaring that I would not open this file on my computer until I had answered my surge of doubt. This final chapter, then, is my own apology for this book.

As Christians, we face a constant temptation to separate worship from work, prayer from action, Sunday from Monday, and then to make sure that they do not interfere with one another. We then wrap up our lives inside the church building in emotional cotton balls, and we like to imagine that they do not change and can all be very neat. So long as everything is beautiful and emotionally comforting, then all is well. But questions like intercommunion, which come up from the awkwardness of life, disturb that tranquil scene. How well our liturgy meets the criteria, not of canon law or the demands of the rubrics but of what it *should* be, is a constant question we must ask if we are "to worship in spirit and in truth" (John 4:23, 24). The reason that this issue of intercommunion is so important is that it is the presenting problem that brings before us all the big questions about Christian worship today. It is *not simply* a matter of providing a theologically satisfactory solution to a pastoral problem—the genuine problem presented by Anke de Bernardinis to the pope and that is argued about in thousands of Christian homes each week—even though we do need a solution to this question. And it is *not simply* a matter of finding a pathway across a major barrier between churches that after centuries of conflict are now trying to find ways to live, work, and worship together and where present Catholic practice presents a barrier that so stifles progress. Rather, the issue of intercommunion calls us to ask questions about how well we appreciate the offer of a place at the banquet that Jesus extends to the disciples—especially if we can then turn to another Christian and say "but you may not eat or drink here." Likewise, how well do we appreciate—it is more than a matter of conscious understanding—the eucharistic nature of the Christian banquet—namely, thanking the Father for all his gifts through his Christ in the power of his Spirit, if we are with a community of disciples celebrating the Christian banquet and do not join in the thanksgiving sacrifice of praise and eat and drink with them.

Immediately, I can hear the shouts from the back of the hall: but *they* do not think of *it* as a sacrifice of praise! Well, that might be the case: they too have room for a deeper theology, but they are engaging in the activity in the manner of the disciples of Jesus. But, comes another voice, you can take part without "communicating"! Well, could I take part in thanking God for his gifts, instanced in this food, and in thanking God for the joy of those gifts, instanced in the cup, and then *not* eat and drink? Surely that would be the ritual equivalent of the cynical "thanks but no thanks"! This may be a polite response to a two-sided or false gift from one human to another, but in relation to God it is a blasphemy and a rejection of the creation. But, cried a third objector, is it *really* a thanksgiving, or just prayerful words uttered by confused Christians? If we start to imagine God with some sort of checklist marking off thanksgiving in the name of Jesus against a list of criteria that bishops and theologians have arrived at—a list like that underpinning the 1896 papal document *Apostolicae curae*[2]—then we have remade a Catholic god in our own image and are inviting each group to do likewise. So we could have an Orthodox god, an Episcopalian god, and—the list will be a long one. We must reject such attempts to imagine that the limits and boundaries of our theology somehow mark out real boundaries in the divine. God is always greater.

Liturgia Semper Reformanda

But is this call to a reform of the liturgy justified? Surely the reform occurred; it has happened! We might argue about when it began—a range of dates can be suggested, such as 1969 with the new missal, 1963 with *Sacrosanctum concilium*, 1962 with *Novum rubricarum*, 1955 with the revised Paschal triduum, or even 1903 with the decree on Gregorian chant—or when it ended—with the new missal in 2011, or some later document that was taken to mean that the period of experimentation was over—but it had fixed limits, and we are now back to "normal." But there can never be an end to experimentation because new situations arise, and we are not yet perfect. Only the heavenly liturgy will be complete and perfect; meanwhile, we do the best we can. That means that we acknowledge our limits and failings. Change is the one constant in both life and liturgy. We all recognize the close relationship between the church and

2. See Franklin 1996.

the liturgy—famously expressed in the phrase that "the liturgy is the center and summit of the church's life"—but often fail to see the consequence. Just as we say that "the church is always needing reform and never reformed,"[3] so the liturgy is always needing reform and never reformed.

Why? Because we are limited creatures who learn slowly, because we are creatures of habit who in repetition become lazy in our thinking and doing, and because we are sinful creatures for whom the truth becomes occluded by our selfishness, we need to continually review and renew our worship. The failure to do so can mean that we start falsifying our image of God, betray our vocation in Jesus, and engage in a liturgy whose end is our dearly held beliefs rather than the true God. An example of this too-close identification of our theological formulations with the mystery being explicated is when we are so concerned with the notion of the eucharist "signifying and effecting" the union of love between the Christ and his church that we fail to notice that the entire relationship of the church to its Lord is, for now, one of infinite invitation and partial response. It is the challenge of Christian living that we must all seek to make ever more real our union with the Christ. This is our vocation of discipleship as we move through life, rather than a once-off achievement that is "just there."[4] If we were writing the CV for the church's nature, then the line "union with the Christ" would be placed under the heading "work in progress." Likewise, every doctrinal statement is partial, and while each partial statement may reflect the truth, even those that are true cannot exclude other apparently contradictory statements. Our theology is, before the mystery of God embraced in the paschal mystery, always fragmentary. It can be true that the eucharist "effects and signifies" union, and it can also be true that the union of each and every Christian is, today, partial—and so either all Christians or none can share at the table—and an expression of longing rather than a statement of a fact. As Jean Calvin remarked: "The eucharist is to be experienced rather than analyzed." However, we should note that while the liturgy is always chang-

3. The famous tag: *ecclesia semper reformanda nunquam reformata.*

4. Catholics often point out that some churches confuse their reverence of the Bible—or defending some aspect of it—with the reverence that is due to God alone; the analogous danger for Catholics is giving reverence to a specific ecclesiastically sanctioned doctrinal position rather than a concern with the mystery of which it is a particular witness.

ing—usually imperceptibly for those who take part in it week by week—this awareness of the need for continual liturgical self-reflection by the church is relatively new and, for many, disturbing. Religion, forging identities and links from the past to the present, is often noted as an inherently conservative force in human affairs: the new fangled is ephemeral, while the certainty of the past is an anchor. But this comes into conflict with the Christian vision that we are on a pilgrimage and a golden age is not a past recalled and conjured by ritual, but a future, the heavenly banquet, which is but glimpsed in our banquets now. Liturgy is far more about longing than about nostalgia.

We often confuse our continual need for liturgical reform with a form of antiquarianism analogous to the quest for the earliest church and the earliest form of the biblical text. Those pursuing such quests, so characteristic of the approach following the Reformation, imagined that they were painstakingly reconstructing a pristine church or a perfect gospel text before a dreaded moment when corruption entered the church.[5] Looking backward to earlier forms of the liturgy has certainly been of great benefit in the renewal of the liturgy since Vatican II, *but this backwards glance is not the essence of liturgical reform*. The liturgy has been in need of reform since the middle of the first century when Paul sought to correct the Corinthians' behavior. Our focus is not upon a past moment treated as an ideal, but upon the vision contained within the preaching of Jesus. We reform the liturgy toward a vision of the kingdom: we seek to make it an expression of the Christian dream. It is this reform to what has never been, and which is very "other" to ordinary experience, that is the challenge of "gathering and renewing everything in the Christ as a plan for the fullness of time" (see Eph 1:10)—which in its Latin form (*instaurare omnia in Christo*) has been the motto of liturgical renewal since the time of St. Pius X. It is in this presentation of the vision inherent in the gospel, now experienced in some partial way in liturgy, that is to be found "the shudder," in a Christian and incarnational mode, that so many students of religion have used as a boundary marker between the sacred and the profane.

One definite aspect that our ongoing reform of the liturgy can take today is to address our practice with regard to intercommunion. We

5. O'Loughlin 2012; Parker 1991; J. Z. Smith 1990.

should make an open and public welcome to every baptized person present that this is the moment looking forward to the future banquet when we shall all be one; and we do this so that our practice more closely coheres with what we say about ourselves as "the disciples," "the baptized," and as "the people of God" on our pilgrim journey.

This then involves a shift in the range of metaphors we use to describe our assembly. Until very recently most of the metaphors used of the eucharist have focused on the privilege and wonderful value of the activity and the object. The eucharist, far from being an activity of us pilgrims in communion with Christ, has been an august sacrament into whose presence we might come only with fear; a sense of unworthiness became an index of sanctity, and sanctity and solemnity were often fused in our consciousness. So we spoke of the precious temple, a treasury, a lofty pinnacle. A visit to a church was somehow akin to a visit to a museum: both brought hushed wonder, heightened by warning such as "do not touch," lest we were not sufficiently aware of our surroundings. This range of images reinforces the notion of the eucharist as an existing achievement, and also as an object possessed by the worshippers.

When we change from such august, eminent metaphors to discipleship, pilgrim metaphors, it becomes possible for us to engage with the issues around intercommunion far more fruitfully because they emphasize the provisional nature of what we do in the earthly liturgy and that liturgy is an activity of the church seeking to be the church. An obvious one is that the liturgy is the school of discipleship: we are not graduates but people who are growing, and we know that our present vision is limited but we look to seeing more and more clearly, and we know that we must be involved in "working on ourselves" if we are to respond to the invitation of faith. We are all learning to be church. Likewise, we can use the metaphor—used by Pope Francis on several occasions—of the field hospital: we have been damaged, and all of us are in need of healing. There is no end to the number of ways we have been damaged and for which we seek the healing power of the Spirit, but one form of damage is particularly relevant to intercommunion. We have, each of us as individuals and as members of churches, been damaged by our inheritance from the history of our churches, the history of sectarian warfare, and the limitations of our own doctrinal understandings. To object to intercommunion is to lock people into their inheritance rather than seeing each of us as needing to have those limitations repaired. A third image is that a gathering of people to celebrate the eucharist is somehow like stopping along a motorway at a service station. It is a place where we get food and drink to give us energy for our journey, a place where we turn aside at regular intervals from our urgent haste and rest. It is where we take stock of where we have got to, check our directions, and set off with new energy. Each gathering, because it is a church, is the host to all who need it—and we would be failing in our duty not to supply anyone in need. But perhaps the most important image is that of "the great party," because this is the image used in Jesus' parables, in the evangelists' preaching, and in the images of the eschaton. The early Christians thought of themselves as being at a festival,[6] and this is an image we should use of ourselves. But if we are the people having a party, can we then go around to some who are at the feast and say: "This food is our source of joy, but it is not for you!"?

Images run together in our minds and form a language that expresses what is possible in our world. When I was boy in the 1960s, the first act of the server was to close the gates of the sanctuary at the altar rails. I already knew I was privileged because a woman, any woman, could not approach that far; at best, a woman could "answer from the rails." Then I crossed another barrier: I had learned, almost by heart and without any understanding, a special language and a set of actions that set me apart from those others who had not done so. The priest saw himself as about to step out of the ordinary world—he was about "to go the altar of God" (Ps 43:4), to the holy of holies[7]—and with every moment the distance was increased. It was a discourse of barriers and barriers are there to be defended: only the rightful get through. The Christ-event is a discourse in the opposite directions: the infinite becomes infant, the temple veil marking off the holy of holies is torn (Mark 15:38 and parallels), and the place of the divine presence becomes the kitchen table. This is the imagery of bridges, making connections, and providing access. The assumption of the bridging images is that you want to encourage communication and communion. This shift in ritual language took physical shape in the early 1970s with the disappearance of gates and rails, and it took verbal shape

6. Wolter 2009.

7. The first phrase, *introibo ad altare Dei*, is taken from the psalm (usually given in its LXX numeration as Ps 42) used as an antiphon in the pre-1970 rite forming one of the prayers at the foot of the altar; the second phrase, *ad Sancta Sanctorum . . . mereamur . . . introire*, from the prayer on ascending to the altar.

with the disappearance of Latin, coupled with the prayers being spoken aloud. Indeed, we could characterize the history of liturgy over the past century as the shift from a cultus of barriers to bridges. Extending our practice of intercommunion is, therefore, going with the grain of the liturgy and its reform.

A Spirituality of the Alternative Table

No theology of the eucharist has ever been developed that did not fit with the great concerns of its time. Perhaps the best example of this is the growth in the metaphysical approach to the eucharist in the twelfth and thirteenth centuries, when a new theology of the eucharist went hand in hand with the recovery of Aristotle in the West. This means that any new approach to intercommunion must be fully coherent with the broader task of setting out our approach to the eucharist today. As we conclude this book, there are three pressing themes that must be explored pastorally in our liturgical practice.

Diversity and Inclusion

For most of our history in the Western church, uniformity was seen as an ideal—and nowhere was uniformity more valued than in the liturgy. This was obviously the case among Catholics whose proud boast was that "from Connemara to Canton" one heard the same words and even the same sounds. But all the established churches expressed this ideal in some way or other: the *Book of Common Prayer* gave expression to the Act of Uniformity, while some of the Scandinavian churches even had their hymns determined centrally. Diversity equalled dissent, and so it was to be excluded. By contrast, there is not a Western institution today that does not pay equal lip service to respecting diversity as an ideal.[8] We want to respect diversity as part of valuing each equally, avoiding various forms of domination by one group over another, and then including those people because exclusion is a form of bullying and control. This theme in contemporary society generates a variety of issues for Catholic liturgy. Some manifestations of this concern are usually embraced without difficulty (such as making adequate provision for those sisters and brothers

8. It would be quite difficult to find a mission statement on any organization's website today that claimed it rejected a respect for diversity.

who are disabled—many buildings have been specially adapted, and in some regions episcopal conferences have given permission for the use of a eucharistic prayer that can easily be signed for the deaf); other areas are virtually closed to discussion (such as women being ordained to preside), but even in these "no-go areas" there is an awareness of the need to address diversity (such as asking women to take on every role except those requiring ordination). Among the issues between these extremes fall those in "irregular" marriage situations, those of differing sexual orientations, and recurring outbreaks of racism or ancient purity cults (such is the caste system in India[9] or prohibitions against menstruating women receiving Communion[10]) that challenge how inclusive our liturgy is or should be. One can gauge how willing any community is to embrace the marginalized by noting which of these areas are problematic and which are not. However, this theme also makes a demand in the ecumenical arena: if we are not seeing the liturgy by analogy with an exclusive uniform club,[11] then we should respect the diversity of theologies in each gathering and then make the gathering an inclusive one. By the very nature of the mission of the Christ, our liturgy cannot be immune to the themes of respecting diversity and practicing inclusion, and intercommunion is a test case whether this is utopian language or part of our real agenda.

Creation Is Gift

If there is a theme surging through mainstream Christian theology today, from Pope Francis's letter *Laudato sí* to notices about the importance of recycling on church notice boards, it is that the material creation is not just "stuff" to be used and discarded but a gift: the reality of God's love around us. This reality forms the basis for both Christian understanding and action, and it is within this perspective that we must view the place of human work. The gifts we offer stand for the Gift, in its totality and in its perfection in the Christ, and they are the earth's fruit and the work of human hands.[12] Therefore, every ecclesial act that offers thanks is a taking part in this drama of creation and redemption. Such an act wells up out of the depths of our identity as Christians, and to imagine it as merely somehow a *potestas*

9. Raj 2014.
10. Berger 2011.
11. See ch. 5 above.
12. See Barclay 2015.

confined within ecclesial ritual structures is not only demeaning but blasphemous for we pray in the Spirit.[13] So when we are developing ever more fruitful theologies of the links between the eucharist and creation, human justice, and ecology, we need to review our own practice when we are among another community celebrating the eucharist.

A Damaged Church

It is only about a single human life span since we confidently compared "The Church"—meaning the Roman Catholic Church—with every other human group and rejoiced that it alone was a *societas perfecta*. While it was not isolated from other Christians, they could only be understood in terms of their relationship to it. It was a dangerous rhetoric that now seems a case ignoring Proverbs 16:18: "Pride goes before destruction, and a haughty spirit before a fall." But it was also fundamentally faulty in that it ignored the in-between, the now and the not yet, nature of the Christian body as a people who journey in pilgrim hope. It also played down the servant aspect of the church within the world, the view that the church exists within human societies and that as the people of God we are continually in need. By an arc of logical inference the "our sins" as individuals was contrasted with the holiness of the "the church"—as in the prayer "Look not on our sins but on the faith of your church"—and then the church was held up as a model for imitation. While the logic is still valid, after two decades of revelations of clergy sexual abuse and scandals of complicity by churches in all manner of moral turpitude, we should be learning a new humility. We may be the church that can claim access to holiness, but any claim to an *intrinsic* holiness employs such an idiosyncratic language game as to be destructive of being taken seriously. Rather, we must acknowledge openly that we are damaged, that we are often shortsighted guides, and we are desperately in need of reconciliation. Once we have made that much-needed admission, then we must offer the welcome of reconciliation as lavishly to anyone else we might

13. There is an old joke told about two chaplains on a warship during World War II: both wanted to reserve the sacrament, but only the Catholic had a tabernacle, and when asked to share it the Catholic replied that such an action was forbidden by naval regulations on storing "live" and "blank" ammunition in the same magazine. This old yarn did accord with *Apostolicae curae*, but it is an interesting exercise in sacramentology to probe why it is faulty and silly.

think as shortsighted as we are. In rejecting intercommunion there is an implicit communication that someone is not up to the mark—and if we set that mark as being aligned on the church subsistent in holiness, unity, and truth, then we are all excluded.

Not only does intercommunion go with the grain of the ongoing process of liturgical reform, it also goes with the grain of the larger calling of the whole church to renew itself in our time.

Two Images—Past and Future

When I was making my First Communion there was a great marble baldachino over the altar, and on it was a mosaic rendering of Leonardo da Vinci's Last Supper. The silent message was that the eucharist was a direct continuity between the pictured and the liturgy—and I am sure that a great many Catholics could give a variant on my experience. This was a very simple message: we have been faithful to the command, change and difference are only in accidentals, and the lines from the past are not only firm but straight. Preaching, teaching, the liturgy itself, and even scholarship further embedded the message. One side effect of this narrative of continuity was that anyone who did not share that image or shared it in some different way—such as a Christian in a church of the Reformation—seemed to be a willful outsider, and this was such a problem that we had to take a very firm line lest the rectitude of the narrative be compromised. Today we should nuance all such simple narratives of continuity, but the image of the Last Supper is firmly fixed in our consciousness, and we invigorate the image every time we say "on the night he was betrayed" within an anaphora. But while a theologian or historian would want to nuance the image on continuity, that does not address its fundamental weakness, which is that the Last Supper image is only half of the story. The eucharist indeed looks backward—but it also looks forward.

The balancing image is of the heavenly banquet, when from north and south and east and west people will have come and are sitting at table in the kingdom of God (Luke 13:29). This image has them enjoying the banquet, and their enjoyment is the new song sung by those ransomed "from every tribe and tongue and people and nation" (Rev 5:9) and, we might add, "and from every church." We need both images balancing one another if we are to locate our liturgy and have the set of benchmarks we need to guide our practice.

Conclusion

Non-Catholics at the Table

Now or Never?

A ritual is "falsified" to the extent to which it cannot serve as a paradigm for significant action outside the ritual itself and is validated to the extent to which it does function in this way.
—Theodore Jennings[1]

Lady van Aefferden wished, not unnaturally, to be buried beside her late husband, Colonel van Gorkum, who had died in 1880, but law and fear of scandal prevented it. She was a Catholic and could not be buried in the Protestant section of the cemetery in the Dutch town of Roermond where he had been interred; she could only await the resurrection alongside fellow Catholics. So before she died she made it clear that she did not want to be buried in her family's tomb; instead she chose a burial plot in the Catholic section of the cemetery as close to her husband's grave as possible. The result is a most unusual pair of tombstones. Set back to back, they clasp hands in stone over the wall that divided the Protestant graves and the Catholic graves. The monument mocked the bitter divisions of the time, and it made a mute but powerful statement that reality is richer and more complex than legally defined borders and categories. Furthermore, given that it is a grave marker, it asserted that Christian divisions are a legacy of past blunders rather than something with

1. Jennings 1982, 119–20.

eschatological reality. This story sums up the fundamental argument of this book: we must adjust our practice in our time rather than wait for the eschaton.

Circular Arguments

I was reminded of these linked tombstones when in 2018 I heard the latest round, this time from Germany, in the search for an answer to the question "Can a non-Catholic share in the table at a Catholic Eucharist?" I have, by the way, used the form "share in the table," because the more common expressions *take communion* or *receive communion* employ the category of the eucharist as a sacred commodity, which Vatican II sought to move beyond in declaring that the eucharist "is an action of Christ himself and the church" (Canon 899.1). The German bishops insisted that "Eucharistic communion and church fellowship belong together," so they could not see any way toward an open invitation. They then fell back on a legal framework of "grave spiritual need," one-off "admittance" using the "internal forum," and leaving it to the discretion of individual bishops. It is all so reminiscent of the debates following *One Bread One Body* in 1998. Apart from the fact that few except canonists understand all the ins and outs of these so-called "solutions," the whole approach leaves many just feeling tired. Some do enjoy using the issue as a political football between liberal and conservative wings of the church; alas, whenever the eucharist is thus used, as it has often been, it is the faith of the whole people of God that suffers. Others, remembering that once you start debating what *grave* means, know that it is no answer at all. Meanwhile those outside Catholicism are often scandalized either by the notion that anyone should act so proprietarily about the table at which all are guests or by the casuistic approach to a mystery. I well remember the Episcopalian shocked at the logic-chopping when told she could not receive in her husband's parish on a Sunday but that she could when holidaying abroad provided she was "morally certain" that she could not find an Episcopal celebration!

This exasperation could be heard in the voice of Anke de Bernardinis, who asked the Pope in 2015 whether there could be movement on sharing the Lord's Supper. The pope's reply was to ask himself: "'Is sharing the Lord's Supper the end of a journey or is it the viaticum for walking together?' I leave the question to the theologians, to those who understand." This is significant in two respects. First, the logic of recent statements is, in effect, eschatological: only when we have perfect communion can we have sacramental sharing—but such fellowship belongs to the same moment on the future horizon when sacraments cease. The pope's mention of *viaticum* and then of a common baptism takes the opposite tack. Second, the widespread opinion that this was a question closed for theological discussion is not one shared by Pope Francis: he explicitly invites new studies of the issue. I hope that in the chapters above, at the very least, these questions and approaches have been given voice.

So what new approaches could be considered?

New Approach 1: Sisters and Brothers in the Spirit

We humans continuously form fictive families. We speak of human fraternity and being welcomed as one of the family. Any nation that speaks of fraternity and equality views itself as a national family, while a great leader is the mother or father of the nation. The language of family is often the highest rhetoric that groupings, large and small, wish to apply to themselves. A monastery is an outstanding case of the fictive family theme with the abbess or abbot (from *abba*, father) and the sisters or brothers. But even these fictive families at the heart of our tradition are but reflections of the fictive family that is the liturgy. There we join as brothers and sisters, act as a family, and are commanded to engage in eucharistic activity as a family: *Orate fratres*. The liturgy-performing family is, to outsiders, simply a ritual manifestation of an anthropological phenomenon. But to us it is the work of the Spirit, who transforms us from being a random collection of individuals with shared ideas into a single family who, as sisters and brothers, cry out "Abba, Father" (Gal 4:6). Our family ties are not merely some legal consequence of our common baptism, but the creating work of the Spirit, there and then, when we actually gather. The transforming Spirit is active in our gatherings, each and every one of them, linking us to every other member of the gathering and empowering our worship.

If the Spirit has made each of us, all baptized, into sisters and brothers, is it appropriate that we would exclude any member of the Spirit-formed family from full participation in the very activity for which the Spirit has transformed us?

New Approach 2: The Grammar of Meals

There are some things in life we cannot change; and facing this fact—as dull as it seems—is, for me, part of being an adult. I must have nourishment and hydration, or I die. But nourishment involves my acting in society: only through human teamwork can we eat. Robinson Crusoe, the ideal individualist, is a great story, but it is entirely fanciful. Just as we work together to gather food, so we collaborate to cook it. If you live alone in a studio apartment, there is still the network that made your microwave oven and generated its electricity! The fact is that humans do not simply eat together, we share meals. Indeed, it is this meal-*sharing* that is distinctively human. We may act in packs as hunter-gatherers, but we eat as meal-sharers with a culture. Moreover, there is an inherent structure to this sharing that we can label the *grammar* of meals. Even in the most elaborate meal with imposed conventions, there are basic codes that are common human property—and when they are transgressed we both know it and know that there is something wrong. A simple example is that we place common food midway between the sharers, we stretch the food so that all get a share, and we have conventions about guests such as the expectation for family members to "hold back."

This has implications for liturgy because the eucharist has, to say the least, the form of a meal, and so the grammar of meals applies. Can I allow you to be present at our meal and then refuse to share the food with you? Can you be at the table and not be offered food to eat and a cup to drink? If you are at the table and refuse my offer, I will be offended and wonder why you are there at all. Likewise, if you are there and express a willingness to eat, then can I be a human host of the divine banquet and respond with what would be brutish behavior anywhere else? Because we confess that we can sit elbow to elbow with the Lord around his eucharistic table, we must accept that the grammar of meals applies there also.

New Approach 3: On Earth, as It Is in Heaven

Each day we pray, in the present tense, that the Father's "will be done on earth, as it is in heaven." Moreover, we see any expression of this will being an anticipation of the eschaton. Constituted as a community of memory, Christianity is unremittingly future focused. What we pray for now is that which we shall enjoy in its fullness in heaven. Moreover, we instantiate this in the eucharist when we refer to it as the "promise" or "taste" of "future glory." We normally think of this relationship in terms of the present leading to the future, but in liturgy—as the sacramental presence of the future now—the future also determines the present.

So, will non-Catholic Christians have a full share in the heavenly banquet? If you answer no, then that solves the problem: they should be excluded now. If you reply yes (see, for example, Matt 8:11 and Luke 13:29), then it is that heavenly table that we should aim to imitate at the gathering next Sunday. Moreover, such an approach would enhance our mission to show that the Good News creates a space of gracious welcome. It would remind us that in the liturgy we perform the unified world that we want to see; we do not simply reinforce the fractured world that we have inherited.

> In the earthly liturgy
> we take part in a foretaste of the heavenly liturgy
> . . . toward which we journey as pilgrims.
> —*Sacrosanctum concilium* 8

Bibliography

Church Documents

Alberigo, J., ed., *Conciliorum Oecumenicorum Decreta*, Basle 1962.

Catholic Bishops' Conferences of England and Wales, Scotland, and Ireland, *One Bread One Body*, London 1998.

The Code of Canon Law in English Translation, London 1983.

Codex Iuris Canonici auctoritate Ioannis Pauli PP. II promulgatus, Vatican 1983.

Denzinger, H., *Enchiridion symbolorum*; see Fastiggi and Englund Nash 2012.

Leo XIII, *Apostolicae curae*; see Franklin 1996.

Sacred Congregation of Rites, *Eucharisticum mysterium*, 1967. See Flannery 1975, 100–136.

Second Vatican Council, *Sacrosanctum concilium*, 1963. See Flannery 1975, 1–40.

World Council of Churches: Faith and Order Commission, *Baptism, Eucharist and Ministry* [Faith and Order Paper 111], Geneva 1982.

Scholarship

Adams, M. McCord, 2010, *Some Later Medieval Theologians on the Eucharist: Thomas Aquinas, Giles of Rome, Duns Scotus, and William of Occam*, Oxford.

Ball, J., 2016, "A reflection on Catholic concerns regarding eucharistic intercommunion among Christians," *One in Christ* 50/1, 45–47.

Barclay, J. M. G., 2015, *Paul and the Gift*, Grand Rapids, MI.

Bates, J. B., 2005, "Giving What Is Sacred to the Dogs? Welcoming All to the Eucharistic Feast," *Journal of Anglican Studies* 3/1, 53–74.

Bauer, W., 1971, *Orthodoxy and Heresy in Earliest Christianity*, Philadelphia [original: *Rechtsgläubigkeit und Ketzerei im ältesten Christentum*, 1934, Tübingen].

Berger, T., 2011, *Gender Differences and the Making of Liturgical History: Lifting a Veil on Liturgy's Past*, Farnham.

Bokser, B. M., 1981, "*Ma'al* and Blessings over Food: Rabbinic Transformation of Cultic Terminology and Alternative Modes of Piety," *Journal of Biblical Literature* 100, 557–74.

———, 1984, *The Origins of the Seder: The Passover Rite and Early Rabbinic Judaism*, New York.
Boyle, L. E., 1982, *The Setting of the* Summa theologiae *of Saint Thomas*, Toronto.
Bradshaw, P. F., 2014, "Ecumenical Participation in Liturgical Translation," in T. O'Loughlin, ed., *Liturgical Language and Translation: The Issues Arising from the Revised English Translation of the Roman Missal*, Norwich, 16–23.
Cassidy, J. M., 2016, "Intercommunion: the Pope and Canon Law," *One in Christ* 50/1, 38–44.
Chadwick, H., 1989, "Ego Berengarius," *Journal of Theological Studies* n.s. 40, 414–45.
Charsley, S. R., 1992, *Wedding Cakes and Cultural History*, London.
Clayton, P. B., 1919, *Tales of Talbot House: Everyman's Club in Poperinghe and Ypres 1915–1918*, London.
Connerton, P., 1989, *How Societies Remember*, Cambridge.
de Vooght, P., 1960, *L'hérésie de Jean Huss*, Leuven.
Diederich, E. A., 1978, "The Unfolding Presence of Christ in the Celebration of Mass," *Communio* 5/4, 326–43.
Dillon, R. J., 1990, "Acts of the Apostles," in R. E. Brown, J. A. Fitzmyer, and R. E. Murphy, eds., *The New Jerome Biblical Commentary*, London, 722–67.
Douglas, M., 1972, "Deciphering a Meal," *Daedalus*, 101, 61–82.
Draper, J. A., 2007, "The Holy Vine of David Made Known to the Gentiles through God's Servant Jesus: 'Christian Judaism' in the *Didache*," in M. Jackson-McCabe, ed., *Jewish Christianity Reconsidered: Rethinking Ancient Groups and Texts*, Minneapolis, 257–83.
Edmonson, S., 2009, "Opening the Table: The Body of Christ and God's Prodigal Grace," *Anglican Theological Review* 91, 213–34.
Ely, J. W. Jr., and D. P. Jordan, 1974, "Harpers Ferry Revisited: Father Costelloe's 'Short Sketch' of Brown's Raid," *Records of the American Catholic Historical Society* 85, 59–67.
Farwell, J., 2004, "Baptism, Eucharist, and the Hospitality of Jesus: On the Practice of 'Open Communion,'" *Anglican Theological Review* 86, 215–38.
———, 2005, "Brief Reflection on Kathryn Tanner's Response to 'Baptism, Eucharist, and the Hospitality of Jesus,'" *Anglican Theological Review* 87, 303–10.
Fastiggi, R., and Englund Nash, A., eds., 2012, *Heinrich Denzinger, Compendium of Creeds, Definitions, and Declarations on Matter of Faith and Morals*, San Francisco [this is the Latin-English edition of Peter Hünermann's forty-third edition of Denzinger's handbook].
Flannery, A., ed., 1975 [2014], *Vatican Council II: The Conciliar and Post-Conciliar Documents*, Collegeville, MN.

Franklin, R. W., ed., 1996, *Anglican Orders: Essays on the Centenary of Apostolicae Curae 1896–1996*, London.

Freestone, W. H., 1917, *The Sacrament Reserved*, London.

Goody, J., 1998, *Food and Love: A Cultural History of East and West*, London and New York.

Jennings, T. W., 1982, "On Ritual Knowledge," *Journal of Religion* 62, 111–27.

Jewett, R., 2007, *Romans: A Commentary*, Minneapolis.

John, H. J., 1966, *The Thomist Spectrum*, New York.

Jones, M., 2007, *Feast: Why Humans Share Food*, Oxford.

Homan, M. M., 2004, "Beer and Its Drinkers: An Ancient Near Eastern Love Story," *Near Eastern Archaeology* 67, 84–95.

Kenrick, F. P., 1860, *Theologia Moralis*, Mechelen [first ed. Philadelphia, 1841].

Knox, R. A., 1950, *Enthusiasm: A Chapter in the History of Religion*, Oxford.

Küng, H., 2002, *My Struggle for Freedom: Memoirs*, Grand Rapids, MI.

Kursawa, W., 2017, *Healing not Punishment: The Historical and Pastoral Networking of the Penitentials between the Sixth and the Eighth Centuries*, Turnhout.

Kuttner, S. G., 1960, *Harmony from Dissonance: An Interpretation of Medieval Canon Law*, Latrobe, PA.

LaPorte, J., 1983, *Eucharistia in Philo*, New York.

Leonhard, C., 2014, "Morning *salutationes* and the Decline of Sympotic Eucharists in the Third Century," *Zeitschrift für antikes Christentum* 18, 420–42.

Lindbeck, G., 1999, "The Eucharist Tastes Bitter in the Divided Church," *Spectrum* 19/1, 1, 4–5.

Lysaght, P., 1991, "'Is There Anyone Here to Serve My Mass?': The Legend of 'The Dead Priest's Midnight Mass' in Ireland," *Arv: Scandinavian Yearbook of Folklore* 47, 193–207.

Macy, G., 1984, *The Theologies of the Eucharist in the Early Scholastic Period: A Study of the Salvific Function of the Sacrament according to the Theologians, c.1080–c.1220*, Oxford.

———, 1992, "Of Mice and Manna: *Quid summit mus?* As a Pastoral Question," *Recherches de Théologie Ancienne et Médiévale* 59, 157–66.

———, 1994, "The Dogma of Transubstantiation in the Middle Ages," *Journal of Ecclesiastical History* 45, 11–41.

Marshall, M., 2009, "'Blessed is anyone who will eat bread in the Kingdom of God': A brief study of Luke 14.15 in its context," in C. M. Tuckett, ed., *Feasts and Festivals*, Leuven, 97–106.

McGowan, A., 2014, *Eucharistic Epicleses, Ancient and Modern: Speaking of the Spirit in Eucharistic Prayer*, London.

McGowan, A. B., 1997, "Naming the feast: The agape and the diversity of early Christian meals," *Studia Patristica* 30, 314–18.

———, 1999, *Ascetic Eucharists: Food and Drink in Early Christian Ritual Meals*, Oxford.
Meyers, R. A., 2012, "Who May Be Invited to the Table?," *Anglican Theological Review* 94, 233–44.
Montinari, M., 2015, *Medieval Tastes: Food, Cooking, and the Table*, New York.
Murphy, J. H., 1961, *The Sacred Ceremonies of Low Mass*, Dublin.
Nichols, B., 2016, "Intercommunion: A Church of England Perspective," *One in Christ* 50/1, 7–21.
Norwood, D. W., 2018, *Pilgrimage of Faith: Introducing the World Council of Churches*, Geneva.
O'Loughlin, T., 2000, "A Woman's Plight and the Western Fathers," in L. J. Kreitzer and D. W. Rooke, eds., *Ciphers in the Sand: Interpretations of The Woman Taken in Adultery (John 7.53–8.11)*, Sheffield, 83–104.
———, 2009, "Another post-resurrection meal, and its implications for the early understanding of the Eucharist," in Z. Rodgers, M. Daly-Denton, and A. Fitzpatrick-McKinley, eds., *A Wandering Galilean: Essays in Honour of Seán Freyne*, Leiden, 485–503.
———, 2009a, "Treating the "Private Mass" as Normal: Some Unnoticed Evidence from Adomnán's *De locis sanctis*," *Archiv für Liturgiewissenschaft* 51, 334–44.
———, 2010, *The Didache: A Window on the Earliest Christians*, London and Grand Rapids, MI.
———, 2010a, "Eucharistic Celebrations: The Chasm between Idea and Reality," *New Blackfriars* 91, 423–38.
———, 2012, "The Prayers of the Liturgy," in V. Boland and T. McCarthy, eds., *The Word is Flesh and Blood: The Eucharist and Sacred Scripture—Festschrift for Prof. Wilfrid Harrington*, Dublin, 113–22.
———, 2012a, "Divisions in Christianity: The Contribution of 'Appeals to Antiquity,' " in S. Oliver, K. Kilby, and T. O'Loughlin, eds., *Faithful Reading: New Essays in Theology and Philosophy in Honour of Fergus Kerr OP*, London, 221–41.
———, 2013, "The Eucharist and the Meals of Jesus," *The Japan Mission Journal* 67/1, 3–11.
———, 2013a, "The Credibility of the Catholic Church as a Public Actor," *New Blackfriars* 94, 129–47.
———, 2014, "The 'Eucharistic Words of Jesus': An Un-noticed Silence in our Earliest Sources," *Anaphora* 8/1, 1–12.
———, 2014a, "Bede's View of the Place of the Eucharist in Anglo-Saxon Life: The Evidence of the *Historia ecclesiastica gentis Anglorum*," in S. Bhattacharji, R. Williams, and D. Mattos, eds., *Prayer and Thought in Monastic Tradition: Essays in Honour of Benedicta Ward S.L.G.*, London, 45–58.

———, 2015, *The Eucharist: Origins and Contemporary Understandings*, London.

———, 2015a, "The Grammar of Meals and the 'Bread of Life,'" *Scripture in Church* 45/179, 117–28.

———, 2016, "Words, Language, Music: Communicating the Word," *Music and Liturgy* 41, 3, 29–38.

———, 2016a, "Theologies of Intercommunion: Responding to a Recent Papal Request," *New Blackfriars* 97, 372–87.

———, 2016b, "Fictive Families—Real Churches: commensality and pneumatology," *One in Christ* 50, 1, 22–37.

———, 2017, "Sacramental Languages and Intercommunion: Identifying a Source of Tension between the Catholic and the Reformed Churches," *Studia Liturgica* 47, 138–50.

———, 2018, "One or Two Cups? The Text of Luke 22:17-20 Again," in H. A. G. Houghton, ed., *The Liturgy and the Living Text of the New Testament: Papers from the Tenth Birmingham Colloquium on the Textual Criticism of the New Testament*, Piscataway, NJ, 51–69.

———, 2018a, *The Rites and Wrongs of Liturgy: Why Good Liturgy Matters*, Collegeville, MN.

Parker, D. C., 1991, "Scripture is Tradition," *Theology* 94, 11–17.

Phillips, L .E., 2005, "Open Tables and Closed Minds," *Liturgy* 20/4, 27–35.

Raj, A. S., 2014, "Dalits at the Eucharistic Table," *The Japan Mission Journal* 68/1, 9–14.

Ratzinger, J., 2000, *The Spirit of the Liturgy*, San Francisco.

Rumsey, P., 2016, "'Though many, we are one bread, one body; for we all partake of the one Bread and one Chalice': Who are you kidding?" *One in Christ* 50/1, 2–6.

Schell, D., 2012, "Discerning the Open Table in Community and Mission," *Anglican Theological Review* 94, 245–55.

Schwartz, B., 1982, "The Social Context of Commemoration: A Study in Collective Memory," *Social Forces* 61, 374–402.

Smit, P.-B., 2011, "A Symposiastic Background to James?," *New Testament Studies* 58, 105–22.

Smith, D. E., 1987, "Table Fellowship as a Literary Motif in the Gospel of Luke," *Journal of Biblical Literature* 106, 613–38.

———, 1989, "The Historical Jesus at Table," in D. J. Lull, ed., *Society of Biblical Literature: 1989 Seminar Papers*, Atlanta, 466–86.

———, 2003, *From Symposium to Eucharist: The Banquet in the Early Christian World*, Minneapolis.

Smith, J. Z., 1990, *Drudgery Divine: On the Comparison of Early Christianities and the Religions of Late Antiquity*, Chicago.

Taft, R. F., 2003, "Mass Without the Consecration? The Historic Agreement on the Eucharist between the Catholic Church and the Assyrian Church of the East Promulgated 26 October 2001," *Worship* 77, 482–509.

Tanner, K., 2004, "In Praise of Open Communion: A Rejoinder to James Farwell," *Anglican Theological Review* 86, 473–85.

Thompson, M. B., 1998, "The Holy Internet: Communication Between Churches in the First Christian Generation," in R. Bauckham, ed., *The Gospels for All Christians: Rethinking Gospel Audiences*, Cambridge, 49–70.

Tracy, D., 1981, *The Analogical Imagination: Christian Theology and the Culture of Pluralism*, London.

Trebilco, P., 2011, "Why Did the Early Christians Call Themselves *he ekklesia*?," *New Testament Studies* 57, 440–60.

Van de Sandt, H., 2002, " 'Do not give what is holy to the dogs' (Did 9:5D and Matt 7:6A): The eucharistic food of the Didache in its Jewish purity setting," *Vigiliae Christianae* 56, 223–46.

Visser, M., 1993, *The Rituals of Dinner: The Origins, Evolution, Eccentricities, and Meaning of Table Manners*, London.

Vogel, C., 1972, "An Alienated Liturgy," *Concilium* 2/8, 11–25.

Wandel, L. P., 2006, *The Eucharist in the Reformation: Incarnation and Liturgy*, Cambridge.

Ware, K., 1978, "Church and Eucharist, Communion and Intercommunion," *Sobornost* 7, 550–67

Whately, R., 1857, *The Scripture Doctrine Concerning the Sacraments and the Points Connected Therewith*, London.

Wilson, A., 2018, *Spirit and Sacrament: An Invitation to Eucharismatic Worship*, Grand Rapids, MI.

Wolter, M., 2009, "Primitive Christianity as a Feast," in C. M. Tuckett, ed., *Feasts and Festivals*, Leuven, 171–82.

Index of Scripture

Index of Subjects

BX 2215.3 .O46 2019
Eating together, becoming one: taking up P
Francis's call to theologians
102694